Fancy Hat
COOKBOOK

Publications International, Ltd.

Favorite Brand Name Recipes at www.fbnr.com

Pictured on the front cover: Berry-Berry Brownie Torte *(page 98)*.

Pictured on the back cover *(clockwise from top):* Chocolate Buttercream Cherry Candies *(page 58)*, Smoked Salmon Roses *(page 56)*, Market Salad *(page 40)* and Josephine's Tea Cakes *(page 60)*.

ISBN: 1-4127-2255-1

Library of Congress Control Number: 2005924033

Manufactured in China.

8 7 6 5 4 3 2 1

Microwave Cooking: Microwave ovens vary in wattage. Use the cooking times as guidelines and check for doneness before adding more time.

Preparation/Cooking Times: Preparation times are based on the approximate amount of time required to assemble the recipe before cooking, baking, chilling or serving. These times include preparation steps such as measuring, chopping and mixing. The fact that some preparations and cooking can be done simultaneously is taken into account. Preparation of optional ingredients and serving suggestions is not included.

Contents

Morning Glory Brunches

Hash Brown Casserole

6 large eggs, well beaten
1 can (12 fluid ounces) NESTLÉ® CARNATION®
   Evaporated Milk
1 teaspoon salt
½ teaspoon ground black pepper
1 package (30 ounces) frozen shredded hash brown potatoes
2 cups (8 ounces) shredded cheddar cheese
1 medium onion, chopped
1 small green bell pepper, chopped
1 cup diced ham (optional)

PREHEAT oven to 350°F. Grease 13×9-inch baking dish.

COMBINE eggs, evaporated milk, salt and black pepper in large bowl. Add potatoes, cheese, onion, bell pepper and ham; mix well. Pour mixture into prepared baking dish.

BAKE for 60 to 65 minutes or until set.   *Makes 12 servings*

Note: For a lower fat version of this recipe, use 3 cartons (4 ounces *each*) cholesterol-free egg product, substitute NESTLÉ® CARNATION® Evaporated Fat Free Milk for Evaporated Milk and 10 slices turkey bacon, cooked and chopped, for the diced ham. Proceed as above.

Hash Brown Casserole

Blueberry White Chip Muffins

2 cups all-purpose flour
½ cup granulated sugar
¼ cup packed brown sugar
2½ teaspoons baking powder
½ teaspoon salt
¾ cup milk
1 large egg, lightly beaten
¼ cup butter or margarine, melted
½ teaspoon grated lemon peel
2 cups (12-ounce package) NESTLÉ® TOLL HOUSE®
    Premier White Morsels, *divided*
1½ cups fresh or frozen blueberries
    Streusel Topping (recipe follows)

PREHEAT oven to 375°F. Paper-line 18 muffin cups.

COMBINE flour, granulated sugar, brown sugar, baking powder and salt in large bowl. Stir in milk, egg, butter and lemon peel. Stir in *1½ cups* morsels and blueberries. Spoon into prepared muffin cups, filling almost full. Sprinkle with Streusel Topping.

BAKE for 22 to 25 minutes or until wooden pick inserted in center comes out clean. Cool in pans for 5 minutes; remove to wire racks to cool slightly.

PLACE *remaining* morsels in small, *heavy-duty* resealable plastic food storage bag. Microwave on MEDIUM-HIGH (70%) power for 30 seconds; knead. Microwave at additional 10- to 15-second intervals, kneading until smooth. Cut tiny corner from bag; squeeze to drizzle over muffins. Serve warm.   *Makes 18 muffins*

Streusel Topping: COMBINE ⅓ cup granulated sugar, ¼ cup all-purpose flour and ¼ teaspoon ground cinnamon in small bowl. Cut in 3 tablespoons butter or margarine with pastry blender or two knives until mixture resembles coarse crumbs.

Blueberry White Chip Muffins

Donna's Heavenly Orange Chip Scones

4 cups all-purpose flour
1 cup granulated sugar
4 teaspoons baking powder
½ teaspoon baking soda
½ teaspoon salt
1 cup (6 ounces) NESTLÉ® TOLL HOUSE® Semi-Sweet
    Chocolate Mini Morsels
1 cup golden raisins
1 tablespoon grated orange peel
1 cup (2 sticks) unsalted butter, cut into pieces and softened
1 cup buttermilk
3 large eggs, *divided*
1 teaspoon orange extract
1 tablespoon milk
   Icing (recipe follows)

PREHEAT oven to 350°F. Lightly grease baking sheets.

COMBINE flour, granulated sugar, baking powder, baking soda and salt in large bowl. Add morsels, raisins and orange peel; mix well. Cut in butter with pastry blender or two knives until mixture resembles coarse crumbs. Combine buttermilk, *2 eggs* and orange extract in small bowl. Pour buttermilk mixture into flour mixture; mix just until a sticky dough is formed. Do not overmix. Drop by ¼ cupfuls onto prepared baking sheets. Combine *remaining* egg and milk in small bowl. Brush egg mixture over top of dough.

BAKE for 18 to 22 minutes or until wooden pick inserted in center comes out clean. For best results, bake one baking sheet at a time. Cool on wire racks for 10 minutes. Drizzle scones with icing. Serve warm.   *Makes 2 dozen scones*

Icing: COMBINE 2 cups powdered sugar, ¼ cup orange juice, 1 tablespoon grated orange peel and 1 teaspoon orange extract in medium bowl. Mix until smooth.

Donna's Heavenly Orange Chip Scones

French Toast Strata

4 ounces day-old French or Italian bread, cut into ¾-inch cubes
    (4 cups)
⅓ cup golden raisins
1 package (3 ounces) cream cheese, cut into ¼-inch cubes
3 eggs
1½ cups milk
½ cup maple-flavored pancake syrup
1 teaspoon vanilla
2 tablespoons sugar
1 teaspoon ground cinnamon
    Additional maple-flavored pancake syrup (optional)

1. Spray 11×7-inch baking dish with nonstick cooking spray. Place bread cubes in even layer in prepared dish; sprinkle raisins and cream cheese evenly over bread.

2. Beat eggs in medium bowl with electric mixer at medium speed until blended. Add milk, ½ cup pancake syrup and vanilla; mix well. Pour egg mixture evenly over bread mixture. Cover; refrigerate at least 4 hours or overnight.

3. Preheat oven to 350°F. Combine sugar and cinnamon in small bowl; sprinkle evenly over strata.

4. Bake, uncovered, 40 to 45 minutes or until puffed, golden brown and knife inserted in center comes out clean. Cut into squares and serve with additional pancake syrup, if desired.   *Makes 6 servings*

Tasty Tip

Model those fancy hats early in the day with a "Hats On Brunch." Serve this hot strata with a fresh fruit compote and crispy bacon—just the right menu to start the day in style!

French Toast Strata

Peach Melba French Toast

French Toast
- 4 BAYS® English Muffins, split
- 3 eggs
- ¾ cup milk or half-and-half
- 2 tablespoons Amaretto liqueur (optional)
- ½ teaspoon vanilla
- ⅛ teaspoon salt
- Dash ground nutmeg
- 4 tablespoons butter or margarine
- ½ pint fresh raspberries
- Confectioners' sugar
- Fresh mint sprigs

Fruit Sauce
- 2 tablespoons butter or margarine
- 4 medium peaches, sliced
- ¾ cup apricot spread or preserves
- 2 tablespoons Amaretto or orange juice

Arrange muffin halves in a large shallow baking dish. In medium bowl, combine eggs, milk, Amaretto, vanilla, salt and nutmeg. Pour over muffins, turning to coat evenly. Cover and refrigerate several hours or overnight.

To cook, heat 2 tablespoons of the butter in a large non-stick skillet. Add 4 muffin halves and cook over medium-high heat until browned, turning once. Remove from skillet and keep warm. Repeat with remaining muffins and butter.

For sauce, heat 2 tablespoons butter in the same skillet. Cook peaches until slightly softened, 2 to 3 minutes. Stir in apricot spread and Amaretto. Heat until mixture bubbles.

To serve, cut French toast slices in half. Arrange 3 pieces on each plate. Spoon some of the peach sauce over each serving. Sprinkle with raspberries and confectioners' sugar. Garnish with mint sprigs, if desired. *Makes 4 to 5 servings*

Peach Melba French Toast

Cherry Orange Poppy Seed Muffins

2 cups all-purpose flour
¾ cup granulated sugar
1 tablespoon baking powder
1 tablespoon poppy seeds
¼ teaspoon salt
1 cup milk
¼ cup (½ stick) butter, melted
1 egg, lightly beaten
½ cup dried tart cherries
3 tablespoons grated orange peel

Combine flour, sugar, baking powder, poppy seeds and salt in large mixing bowl. Add milk, melted butter and egg, stirring just until dry ingredients are moistened. Gently stir in cherries and orange peel. Fill paper-lined muffin cups three-fourths full.

Bake in preheated 400°F oven 18 to 22 minutes or until wooden pick inserted in center comes out clean. Let cool in pan 5 minutes. Remove from pan and serve warm or let cool completely.

Makes 12 muffins

Favorite recipe from **Cherry Marketing Institute**

Mini Turkey Ham Quiche

1 cup JENNIE-O TURKEY STORE® Turkey Ham, diced
¾ cup cheddar cheese shredded
3 (6-inch) unbaked frozen pie shells
3 eggs, beaten
¾ cup skim milk

Preheat oven to 350°F. Sprinkle turkey ham and cheese over pie shell. In small bowl, combine egg and milk; pour evenly into pie shell. On cookie sheet, bake quiche 20 to 25 minutes or until knife inserted in center comes out clean.

Makes 3 servings

Prep Time: 15 minutes
Cook Time: 30 minutes

Cherry Orange Poppy Seed Muffins

Delicious Ham & Cheese Puff Pie

2 cups (about 1 pound) diced cooked ham
1 package (10 ounces) frozen chopped spinach, thawed
    and squeezed dry
½ cup diced red bell pepper
4 green onions, sliced
3 eggs
¾ cup all-purpose flour
¾ cup (3 ounces) shredded Swiss cheese
¾ cup milk
1 tablespoon prepared mustard
1 teaspoon grated lemon peel
1 teaspoon dried dill weed
½ teaspoon garlic salt
½ teaspoon black pepper
    Dill sprigs and lemon slices (optional)

1. Preheat oven to 425°F. Grease round 2-quart casserole.

2. Combine ham, spinach, bell pepper and onions in prepared casserole.

3. Beat eggs in medium bowl. Stir in remaining ingredients; pour over ham mixture.

4. Bake 30 to 35 minutes or until puffed and browned. Cut into wedges and garnish with dill sprigs and lemon slices, if desired.

Makes 4 to 6 servings

Tasty Tip

Brunches can be a breeze to prepare and fun to serve. Measure the ingredients and set the table the night before. Spice up your place settings with brightly colored napkins and flowers. In the morning, warm a variety of breads and prepare lots of coffee and tea. Then, put on your fancy attire and hat. Let the merriment begin!

Delicious Ham & Cheese Puff Pie

Orange Cinnamon Swirl Bread

Bread
1 package DUNCAN HINES® Bakery-Style Cinnamon Swirl Muffin Mix
1 egg
⅔ cup orange juice
1 tablespoon grated orange peel

Orange Glaze
½ cup confectioners' sugar
2 to 3 teaspoons orange juice
1 teaspoon grated orange peel
Quartered orange slices for garnish (optional)

1. Preheat oven to 350°F. Grease and flour 8½×4½×2½-inch loaf pan.

2. For bread, combine muffin mix and contents of topping packet from mix in large bowl. Break up any lumps. Add egg, ⅔ cup orange juice and 1 tablespoon orange peel. Stir until moistened, about 50 strokes. Knead swirl packet from mix for 10 seconds before opening. Squeeze contents on top of batter. Swirl into batter with knife or spatula, folding from bottom of bowl to get an even swirl. *Do not completely mix in.* Pour into prepared pan. Bake at 350°F for 55 to 60 minutes or until toothpick inserted in center comes out clean. Cool in pan 10 minutes. Loosen loaf from pan. Invert onto cooling rack. Turn right side up. Cool completely.

3. For orange glaze, place confectioners' sugar in small bowl. Add orange juice, 1 teaspoon at a time, stirring until smooth and of desired consistency. Stir in 1 teaspoon orange peel. Drizzle over loaf. Garnish with orange slices, if desired. *Makes 1 loaf (12 slices)*

Tip: If glaze becomes too thin, add more confectioners' sugar. If glaze is too thick, add more orange juice.

Orange Cinnamon Swirl Bread

Donut Spice Cakes

1 package (9 ounces) yellow cake mix
½ cup cold water
2 eggs
½ teaspoon ground cinnamon
¼ teaspoon ground nutmeg
2 teaspoons powdered sugar

1. Preheat oven to 350°F. Grease and flour 10 (½-cup) mini Bundt pans.

2. Combine cake mix, water, eggs, cinnamon and nutmeg in medium bowl. Beat with electric mixer at high speed 4 minutes or until well blended.

3. Spoon about ¼ cup batter into each prepared Bundt pan cup. Bake 13 minutes or until toothpicks inserted into centers come out clean and cakes spring back when lightly touched.

4. Cool in pans on wire racks 5 minutes. Remove cakes from pans. Serve warm or at room temperature. Sprinkle with powdered sugar just before serving. *Makes 10 servings*

Overnight Ham and Cheese Strata

12 slices white bread, crusts removed
1 (10-ounce) package frozen chopped broccoli, thawed
    and drained
2 (5-ounce) cans HORMEL® chunk ham, drained and flaked
6 eggs, beaten
2 cups milk
¼ cup minced onion
¼ teaspoon dry mustard
3 cups shredded Cheddar cheese

Cut bread into small cubes. Layer one-half of bread cubes, broccoli and chunk ham in buttered 13×9-inch baking dish. Top with remaining bread cubes. Beat together eggs, milk, onion and dry mustard. Pour over bread. Sprinkle top with cheese. Cover and refrigerate overnight. Heat oven to 325°F. Bake 55 to 60 minutes or until eggs are set. *Makes 12 servings*

Donut Spice Cakes

Smoked Cheese and Muffin Strata

6 BAYS® English Muffins, cubed
8 ounces smoked Gouda cheese, sliced
8 ounces Cheddar cheese, sliced
8 ounces pork or turkey bulk sausage, cooked and crumbled
4¾ cups milk
8 eggs
⅓ cup diced red pepper
⅓ cup diced green pepper
1 teaspoon salt
Pinch ground black pepper
Paprika, to taste

Line bottom of 13×9-inch pan with half of the muffin cubes. Divide cheeses evenly over muffin cubes in pan. Sprinkle on crumbled sausage. Arrange remaining muffin cubes in pan over sausage and cheese layers.

Mix together milk, eggs, peppers, salt and black pepper. Pour over ingredients in pan. Press down on muffin cubes to soak thoroughly. Sprinkle with paprika. Cover with plastic. Refrigerate 8 hours or overnight.

Bake uncovered in 325°F oven for just over 2 hours or until a knife inserted near the center comes out clean. Let stand 5 minutes before serving. *Makes 6 servings*

Note: Recipe may be halved. Bake in an 8-inch square pan for 1 hour and 15 minutes or until a knife inserted near center comes out clean.

Smoked Cheese and Muffin Strata

Banana Bread Waffles with Cinnamon Butter

½ cup unsalted whipped butter, softened
2 tablespoons powdered sugar
2 teaspoons grated orange peel
¼ teaspoon ground cinnamon
¼ teaspoon vanilla
1 package (7 ounces) banana muffin mix
⅔ cup buttermilk
1 egg
   Nonstick cooking spray

1. Preheat waffle iron.

2. Combine butter, powdered sugar, orange peel, cinnamon and vanilla in small bowl; mix well. Set aside.

3. Combine muffin mix, buttermilk and egg in medium bowl; stir until just blended.

4. Spray waffle iron with cooking spray. Spoon about ¾ cup batter* onto iron. Close lid; bake until steaming stops or waffles are brown and crispy.

5. Spoon equal amounts butter mixture onto each waffle.

Makes 4 servings

Check the manufacturer's directions for recommended amount of batter and baking time.

Tasty Tip

Everyone loves waffles! To serve waffles to a group, put the waffle iron on a heat proof tray on a small side table or cart next to the dining table. Cook the waffles—hot and fresh—right at the table. Or, prepare the waffles just before serving. Keep warm and crispy by putting them directly on the oven rack in a 250°F oven.

Banana Bread Waffles with Cinnamon Butter

Red-Hot Diva Luncheons

Crab-Artichoke Casserole

8 ounces uncooked small shell pasta
2 tablespoons butter
6 green onions, chopped
2 tablespoons all-purpose flour
1 cup half-and-half
1 teaspoon dry mustard
½ teaspoon ground red pepper
   Salt and black pepper
½ cup (2 ounces) shredded Swiss cheese, divided
1 package (about 8 ounces) imitation crabmeat chunks
1 can (about 14 ounces) artichoke hearts, drained and cut into
   bite-size pieces

1. Preheat oven to 350°F. Grease 2-quart casserole. Cook pasta according to package directions; drain and set aside.

2. Heat butter in large saucepan over medium heat; add green onions. Cook and stir about 2 minutes. Add flour; cook and stir 2 minutes more. Gradually add half-and-half, whisking constantly until mixture begins to thicken. Whisk in mustard and red pepper; season to taste with salt and black pepper. Remove from heat and stir in ¼ cup cheese until melted.

3. Combine crabmeat, artichokes and pasta in casserole. Add sauce mixture and stir well. Top with remaining ¼ cup cheese. Bake about 40 minutes or until hot, bubbly and lightly browned.

Makes 6 servings

Crab-Artichoke Casserole

Hula Chicken Salad
with Orange Poppy Seed Dressing

½ cup prepared vinaigrette salad dressing
¼ cup *French's*® Honey Dijon Mustard
1 tablespoon grated orange peel
1 tablespoon water
1 teaspoon poppy seeds
1 pound chicken tenders
1 tablespoon jerk seasoning
8 cups cut-up romaine lettuce
3 cups cut-up fruit from salad bar such as oranges, melon, strawberries, pineapple

1. Combine salad dressing, mustard, orange peel, water and poppy seeds; mix well. Reserve.

2. Rub chicken tenders with jerk seasoning. Skewer chicken and grill over medium-high heat until no longer pink, about 5 minutes per side.

3. Arrange lettuce and fruit on salad plates. Top with chicken and serve with dressing. *Makes 4 servings*

Prep Time: 15 minutes
Cook Time: 10 minutes

Tasty Tip

Oh my! It's your turn to serve lunch. Make this salad in a snap by purchasing cut up fruit and prepackaged lettuce. Dress to the nines in your diva attire. Then, assemble the salad just before serving. They'll rave about the Hula Chicken.

Hula Chicken Salad with Orange Poppy Seed Dressing

Cheesy Broccoli Bake

1 (10-ounce) package frozen chopped broccoli
1 (10¾-ounce) can condensed Cheddar cheese soup
½ cup sour cream
2 cups (12 ounces) chopped CURE 81® ham
2 cups cooked rice
½ cup soft, torn bread crumbs
1 tablespoon butter or margarine, melted

Heat oven to 350°F. Cook broccoli according to package directions; drain. Combine soup and sour cream. Stir in broccoli, ham and rice. Spoon into 1½-quart casserole. Combine bread crumbs and butter; sprinkle over casserole. Bake 30 to 35 minutes or until thoroughly heated. *Makes 4 to 6 servings*

Chicken Enchiladas

2 tablespoons vegetable oil
1 medium onion, chopped
3 to 4 cups cooked, shredded chicken or turkey
1 can (14½ ounces) diced tomatoes, in juice
1 can (8 ounces) tomato sauce
1 can (4 ounces) diced green chiles
1 package (1.0 ounce) LAWRY'S® Taco Spices & Seasonings
½ teaspoon LAWRY'S® Seasoned Salt
¼ teaspoon LAWRY'S® Garlic Powder With Parsley
1 dozen corn tortillas
2 cans (2¼ ounces each) sliced black olives, drained
5 cups (20 ounces) shredded Monterey Jack cheese

In large skillet, heat oil. Add onion and cook over medium-high heat until tender. Add chicken, tomatoes, tomato sauce, chiles, Taco Spices & Seasonings, Seasoned Salt and Garlic Powder With Parsley; mix well. Bring to a boil; reduce heat to low, cover and cook for 15 to 20 minutes. In greased 13×9×2-inch baking dish, place 4 corn tortillas. Pour ⅓ of chicken mixture over tortillas, spreading evenly. Layer with ⅓ of olives and ⅓ of cheese. Repeat layers 2 times ending with cheese. Bake, uncovered, in 350°F oven for 30 to 40 minutes; until chicken is thoroughly cooked. *Makes 6 to 8 servings*

Cheesy Broccoli Bake

Turkey, Mandarin and Poppy Seed Salad

¼ cup orange juice
1½ tablespoons red wine vinegar
1½ teaspoons poppy seeds
1½ teaspoons olive oil
1 teaspoon Dijon-style mustard
⅛ teaspoon black pepper
5 cups torn stemmed washed red leaf lettuce
2 cups torn stemmed washed spinach
½ pound honey roasted turkey breast, cut into ½-inch strips
1 can (10½ ounces) mandarin oranges, drained

In small bowl, combine orange juice, vinegar, poppy seeds, oil, mustard and pepper. Set aside. In large bowl, toss together lettuce, spinach, turkey and oranges. Pour dressing over turkey mixture and serve immediately. *Makes 4 servings*

Favorite recipe from **National Turkey Federation**

Turkey Divan

2 cups cubed JENNIE-O TURKEY STORE® Fully Cooked Oven-Roasted Turkey Breast
2 packages (10 ounces each) frozen asparagus or broccoli spears, thawed
1 cup shredded Swiss cheese, divided
⅓ cup sliced green onions
1 tablespoon vegetable oil
2 teaspoons cornstarch
1 cup milk
1 HERB-OX® chicken flavored instant bouillon cube or packet
1 teaspoon dry mustard

Heat oven to 350°F. Arrange asparagus in greased 9×9-inch baking pan. Sprinkle with ½ cup cheese. Layer turkey on top. In small saucepan over medium heat, cook green onion in oil until tender. Stir in cornstarch. Add milk. Cook and stir 3 minutes or until thickened. Cook and stir 3 minutes longer. Stir in bouillon and dry mustard. Stir in remaining ½ cup cheese. Pour sauce over turkey. Bake 20 minutes or until golden brown. *Makes 4 servings*

Turkey, Mandarin and Poppy Seed Salad

Quick Chicken Pot Pie

1 pound boneless skinless chicken thighs, cut into 1-inch cubes
1 can (about 14 ounces) chicken broth
3 tablespoons all-purpose flour
2 tablespoons butter, softened
1 package (10 ounces) frozen mixed vegetables, thawed
1 can (about 4 ounces) button mushrooms, drained
¼ teaspoon dried basil leaves
¼ teaspoon dried oregano leaves
¼ teaspoon dried thyme leaves
1 cup biscuit baking mix
6 tablespoons milk

1. Preheat oven to 450°F. Grease 2-quart casserole.

2. Place chicken and broth in large skillet. Cover; bring to a boil over high heat. Reduce heat to medium. Simmer, uncovered, 5 minutes or until chicken is tender.

3. Combine flour and butter; set aside. Combine mixed vegetables, mushrooms, basil, oregano and thyme in prepared casserole.

4. Whisk flour mixture into chicken and broth in skillet. Cook and stir until smooth and thickened. Add to vegetable mixture; mix well.

5. Blend biscuit mix and milk in medium bowl until smooth. Drop 4 scoops batter onto chicken mixture.

6. Bake 18 to 20 minutes or until biscuits are browned and casserole is hot and bubbly. *Makes 4 servings*

This dish can be prepared ahead through step 4. Cover and refrigerate up to 24 hours. Proceed with step 5 and bake as directed for 20 to 25 minutes.

Quick Chicken Pot Pie

Tropical Curried Chicken Salad

⅔ cup prepared olive oil vinaigrette salad dressing
¼ cup *French's®* Worcestershire Sauce
¼ cup honey
2 tablespoons *Frank's®* *RedHot®* Cayenne Pepper Sauce
2 teaspoons curry powder
2 cloves garlic, minced
1 pound boneless, skinless chicken breasts
8 cups washed and torn watercress and Boston lettuce
¼ cup coarsely chopped unsalted cashew nuts
½ cup shredded coconut, toasted

1. Place salad dressing, Worcestershire, honey, *Frank's®* *RedHot®* Sauce, curry and garlic in blender or food processor. Cover; process until well blended. Reserve ½ cup curry mixture to dress salad.

2. Place chicken in large resealable plastic food storage bag. Pour remaining curry mixture over chicken. Seal bag; marinate in refrigerator 30 minutes.

3. Heat electric grill pan or barbecue grill. Grill chicken 10 to 15 minutes or until no longer pink in center. Arrange salad greens on large serving platter. Cut chicken into thin slices. Arrange over greens. Top with nuts and coconut. Serve with reserved dressing.

Makes 4 servings

Prep Time: 15 minutes
Cook Time: 15 minutes
Marinate Time: 30 minutes

Tropical Curried Chicken Salad

Pesto Lasagna

1 package (16 ounces) uncooked lasagna noodles
3 tablespoons olive oil
1½ cups chopped onion
3 cloves garlic, finely chopped
3 packages (10 ounces each) frozen chopped spinach, thawed
    and squeezed dry
    Salt
    Black pepper
3 cups (24 ounces) ricotta cheese
1½ cups prepared pesto sauce
¾ cup (3 ounces) grated Parmesan cheese
½ cup pine nuts, toasted
6 cups (16 ounces) shredded mozzarella cheese
    Strips of roasted red pepper (optional)

1. Preheat oven to 350°F. Oil 13×9-inch casserole or lasagna pan. Partially cook lasagna noodles according to package directions.

2. Heat oil in large skillet. Cook and stir onion and garlic until transparent. Add spinach; cook and stir about 5 minutes. Season with salt and pepper. Transfer to large bowl.

3. Add ricotta cheese, pesto, Parmesan cheese and pine nuts to spinach mixture; mix well.

4. Layer 5 lasagna noodles, slightly overlapping, in prepared casserole. Top with ⅓ of spinach-ricotta mixture and ⅓ of mozzarella. Repeat layers twice.

5. Bake about 35 minutes or until hot and bubbly. Garnish with red pepper, if desired.

Makes 8 servings

Pesto Lasagna

Warm Chutney Chicken Salad

Nonstick olive oil cooking spray
6 ounces boneless skinless chicken breasts,
    cut into bite-size pieces
1/3 cup mango chutney
1/4 cup water
1 tablespoon Dijon mustard
4 cups packaged mixed salad greens
1 cup chopped peeled mango or papaya
Sliced green onions (optional)

1. Spray medium nonstick skillet with cooking spray. Heat over medium-high heat. Add chicken; cook and stir 2 to 3 minutes or until no longer pink. Stir in chutney, water and mustard. Cook and stir just until hot. Cool slightly.

2. Toss together salad greens and mango. Arrange on serving plates.

3. Spoon chicken mixture onto greens. Garnish with green onions, if desired.   *Makes 2 servings*

Market Salad

3 eggs
4 cups washed mixed baby salad greens
2 cups green beans, cut into 1½-inch pieces, cooked and drained
4 thick slices bacon, crisp-cooked, drained and crumbled
1 tablespoon minced fresh basil, chives or Italian parsley
3 tablespoons olive oil
1 tablespoon red wine vinegar
1 teaspoon Dijon mustard
1/4 teaspoon salt
1/4 teaspoon pepper

1. Place eggs in small pot with water to cover. Bring to a boil over medium-high heat. Immediately remove from heat. Cover; let rest 10 minutes. Drain; cool eggs to room temperature.

2. Combine salad greens, green beans, bacon and basil in large salad bowl. Peel and coarsely chop eggs; stir into salad. Combine oil, vinegar, mustard, salt and pepper in small bowl; drizzle over salad. Toss gently but thoroughly.   *Makes 4 servings*

Warm Chutney Chicken Salad

Spinach Quiche

1 medium leek
¼ cup (½ stick) butter
2 cups finely chopped cooked chicken
½ (10-ounce) package frozen chopped spinach or broccoli,
    cooked and drained
1 unbaked ready-to-use pie crust (10 inches in diameter)
1½ cups (6 ounces) shredded Swiss cheese
1 tablespoon all-purpose flour
1½ cups half-and-half or evaporated milk
4 eggs
2 tablespoons brandy
½ teaspoon salt
¼ teaspoon black pepper
¼ teaspoon ground nutmeg

1. Preheat oven to 375°F. Cut leek in half lengthwise; wash and trim,
leaving 2 to 3 inches of green tops intact. Cut leek halves crosswise
into thin slices. Place in small saucepan; add enough water to cover.
Bring to a boil over high heat; reduce heat and simmer 5 minutes.
Drain; reserve leek.

2. Melt butter in large skillet over medium heat. Add chicken; cook
5 minutes or until chicken is golden. Add spinach and leek to chicken
mixture; cook 1 to 2 minutes longer. Remove from heat. Spoon mixture
into unbaked pie crust; sprinkle with cheese and flour.

3. Combine half-and-half, eggs, brandy, salt, pepper and nutmeg in
medium bowl; pour over cheese.

4. Bake 35 to 40 minutes or until knife inserted into center comes out
clean. Let stand 5 minutes before serving. Serve hot or cold.

Makes 6 servings

Spinach Quiche

Near East Steak Salad

⅔ cup *French's*® Honey Dijon Mustard
½ cup water
¼ cup teriyaki sauce
2 tablespoons grated peeled ginger
1 teaspoon minced garlic
1 pound boneless sirloin or flank steak (1-inch thick)
8 cups mixed salad greens, washed and torn
1 medium yellow or orange bell pepper, thinly sliced
2 green onions, thinly shredded
¼ cup chopped dry roasted peanuts

1. Combine mustard, water, teriyaki sauce, ginger and garlic in small bowl. Pour 1 cup dressing into small serving bowl.

2. Broil or grill steak 10 minutes or until desired doneness, basting with remaining ½ cup dressing. Let stand 5 minutes.

3. Thinly slice steak. Serve over salad greens. Top with bell pepper, green onions and peanuts. Drizzle with reserved dressing.

Makes 4 servings

Prep Time: 10 minutes
Cook Time: 10 minutes

Wilted Spinach Mandarin

1 tablespoon oil
½ pound fresh spinach, washed and stemmed
1 cup bean sprouts
1 can (11 ounces) mandarin oranges, drained
2 tablespoons reduced-sodium soy sauce
2 tablespoons orange juice
Quartered orange slices for garnish

Heat oil in wok or large skillet over medium-high heat. Add spinach, bean sprouts and mandarin oranges to wok. Stir-fry 1 to 2 minutes just until spinach wilts. Transfer to serving dish. Heat soy sauce and orange juice in wok; pour over spinach and toss gently to coat. Garnish, if desired.

Makes 4 side-dish servings

Near East Steak Salad

Chicken Tuscany

6 medium red potatoes, scrubbed and sliced ⅛ inch thick
12 ounces shiitake, cremini, chanterelle and/or button mushrooms,
   sliced
4 tablespoons olive oil, divided
4 tablespoons grated Parmesan cheese, divided
3 teaspoons minced garlic, divided
3 teaspoons minced fresh rosemary *or* 1½ teaspoons dried
   rosemary leaves, divided
  Salt and ground pepper
1 package (about 3 pounds) PERDUE® Fresh Pick of the
  Chicken

Preheat oven to 425°F. Pat potatoes dry with paper towels. Toss
potatoes and mushrooms with 2½ tablespoons oil, 2 tablespoons
cheese, 2 teaspoons garlic, 2 teaspoons rosemary, ½ teaspoon salt and
¼ teaspoon pepper. In 13×9-inch baking dish, arrange potatoes in one
layer; top with remaining 2 tablespoons cheese. Bake 15 minutes or
until potatoes are lightly browned; set aside.

Meanwhile, in large nonstick skillet over medium heat, heat remaining
1½ tablespoons oil. Add chicken pieces. Season lightly with salt and
pepper; sprinkle with remaining rosemary and garlic. Cook chicken
5 to 6 minutes on each side or until browned. (Do not crowd pan; if
necessary, brown chicken in two batches.)

Arrange chicken on top of potato mixture; drizzle with any oil from
skillet and return to oven. Bake 20 to 25 minutes longer or until
chicken is no longer pink in center. Serve chicken, potatoes and
mushrooms with green salad, if desired.   *Makes 6 servings*

Chicken Tuscany

Spicy Thai Warm Shrimp Salad

¾ cup prepared vinaigrette salad dressing
⅓ cup chopped fresh mint leaves
¼ cup *Frank's® RedHot®* XTRA Hot Sauce or *Frank's® RedHot®*
    Cayenne Pepper Sauce
¼ cup *French's®* Honey Dijon Mustard
1 tablespoon lime juice
1 tablespoon sucralose sugar substitute
1 tablespoon vegetable oil
1½ pounds large shrimp, shelled with tails left on
8 cups shredded Napa cabbage
1 red bell pepper, thinly sliced
1 cup thinly sliced cucumber

1. Combine salad dressing, mint, XTRA Hot Sauce, mustard, lime juice and sugar substitute in large bowl; set aside.

2. Heat oil in large nonstick skillet or wok until hot. Stir-fry shrimp 2 to 3 minutes until shrimp turn pink. Transfer to bowl with dressing. Add cabbage, bell pepper and cucumber; toss to coat. Serve warm.

Makes 6 servings

Prep Time: 10 minutes
Cook Time: 5 minutes

Tasty Tip

Send out extravagant invitations and let the fun begin. This red-hot spicy salad is perfect for a spectacular luncheon. Add delicious bread and a creamy cool royal dessert. Don't forget to leave enough free time to get dressed in your outrageous luncheon outfit.

Spicy Thai Warm Shrimp Salad

Tortellini with Artichokes, Olives and Feta Cheese

2 packages (9 ounces) refrigerated cheese-filled spinach tortellini
2 jars (4 ounces) marinated artichoke heart quarters, drained*
½ cup sliced pitted ripe olives
2 medium carrots, diagonally sliced
½ cup (2 ounces) crumbled feta cheese
½ cup cheese-garlic Italian salad dressing
    Black pepper

*For additional flavor, add some artichoke marinade to tortellini with salad dressing.

1. Cook pasta according to package directions. Rinse under cold water until pasta is cool; drain.

2. Combine pasta, artichoke hearts, olives, carrots and feta cheese in large bowl. Add salad dressing; toss lightly. Season to taste with black pepper.   *Makes 6 servings*

Serving Suggestions: Serve with whole-wheat dinner rolls and fresh melons such as honeydew, watermelon, cantaloupe or Crenshaw.

Prep and Cook Time: 23 minutes

Tasty Tip

Pasta salad , warm wheat rolls and juicy fresh fruit is the perfect menu for a Healthful Red-Hot Diva Luncheon. Come attired in stylish and comfortable warm ups. Hats on for an invigorating after lunch walk.

Tortellini with Artichokes, Olives and Feta Cheese

Southwest Grilled Pork Salad

½ cup *French's® Gourmayo™* Smoked Chipotle Light Mayonnaise
¼ cup orange juice
1 teaspoon grated orange peel
4 teaspoons chili powder
1 teaspoon salt
4 boneless pork chops (1-inch thick) or chicken breasts
8 cups baby spinach leaves or mixed field greens
2 oranges, cut into sections
1½ cups julienned, peeled jicama*
1 cup *French's®* French Fried Onions or *French's®* Cheddar
French Fried Onions

Note: Jicama is a root vegetable with a thick brown skin and crunchy, sweet flesh. It may be eaten raw or cooked. It can be purchased in most supermarkets or Mexican markets. Canned, sliced water chestnuts may be substituted.

1. Combine mayonnaise, juice and orange peel in small bowl; set aside. Rub chili powder and salt into pork, coating all sides.

2. Grill or broil pork over medium-high heat until no longer pink in center. Cut pork into ½-inch cubes.

3. Arrange spinach, oranges and jicama on serving plates. Top with pork and serve with dressing. Sprinkle with French Fried Onions.

Makes 4 servings

Prep Time: 10 minutes
Cook Time: 15 minutes

Southwest Grilled Pork Salad

Chicken Pot Pie with Onion Biscuits

1 package (1.8 ounces) classic white sauce mix
2¾ cups milk, divided
¼ teaspoon dried thyme leaves
1 package (10 ounces) frozen peas and carrots, thawed
1 package (10 ounces) roasted carved chicken breast, cut into bite-size pieces
1 cup all-purpose baking mix
1⅓ cups *French's*® French Fried Onions, divided
½ cup (2 ounces) shredded Cheddar cheese

1. Preheat oven to 400°F. Prepare white sauce mix according to package directions with 2¼ cups milk; stir in thyme. Mix vegetables, chicken and prepared white sauce in shallow 2-quart casserole.

2. Combine baking mix, ⅔ *cup* French Fried Onions and remaining ½ cup milk in medium bowl until blended. Drop 6 to 8 spoonfuls of dough over chicken mixture.

3. Bake 25 minutes or until biscuits are golden. Sprinkle biscuits with cheese and remaining onions. Bake 3 minutes or until cheese is melted and onions are golden. *Makes 6 servings*

Tip: You may substitute 2 cups cut-up cooked chicken for the roasted, carved chicken breast.

Variation: For added Cheddar flavor, substitute *French's*® **Cheddar French Fried Onions** for the original flavor.

Prep Time: 15 minutes
Cook Time: 33 minutes

Chicken Pot Pie with Onion Biscuits

High-Hat Tea Parties

Smoked Salmon Roses

1 package (8 ounces) cream cheese, softened
1 tablespoon prepared horseradish
1 tablespoon minced fresh dill plus whole sprigs for garnish
1 tablespoon half-and-half
16 slices (12 to 16 ounces) smoked salmon
1 red bell pepper, cut into thin strips

1. Combine cream cheese, horseradish, minced dill and half-and-half in small bowl. Beat until light and creamy.

2. Spread 1 tablespoon cream cheese mixture over each salmon slice. Roll up jelly-roll fashion. Slice each roll in half crosswise. Arrange salmon rolls, cut sides down, on serving dish to resemble roses. Garnish each "rose" by tucking 1 pepper strip and 1 dill sprig in center. *Makes 32 servings*

Smoked Salmon Roses

Chocolate Buttercream
Cherry Candies

About 48 maraschino cherries with stems, well drained
1/4 cup (1/2 stick) butter, softened
2 cups powdered sugar
1/4 cup HERSHEY'S Cocoa or HERSHEY'S Dutch Processed
    Cocoa
1 to 2 tablespoons milk, divided
1/2 teaspoon vanilla extract
1/4 teaspoon almond extract
    White Chip Coating (recipe follows)
    Chocolate Chip Drizzle (recipe follows)

1. Cover tray with wax paper. Lightly press cherries between layers of paper towels to remove excess moisture.

2. Beat butter, powdered sugar, cocoa and 1 tablespoon milk in small bowl until well blended; stir in vanilla and almond extract. If necessary, add remaining milk, one teaspoon at a time, until mixture will hold together but is not wet.

3. Mold scant teaspoon mixture around each cherry, covering completely; place on tray. Cover; refrigerate 3 hours or until firm.

4. Prepare White Chip Coating. Holding each cherry by stem, dip into coating. Place on tray; refrigerate until firm.

5. About 1 hour before serving, prepare Chocolate Chip Drizzle; with tines of fork drizzle randomly over candies. Refrigerate until drizzle is firm. Store in refrigerator.   *Makes about 48 candies*

White Chip Coating: Place 2 cups (12-ounce package) HERSHEY'S Premier White Chips in small microwave-safe bowl; drizzle with 2 tablespoons vegetable oil. Microwave at HIGH (100%) 1 minute; stir. If necessary, microwave at HIGH an additional 15 seconds at a time, stirring after each heating just until chips are melted and mixture is smooth. If mixture thickens while coating, microwave at HIGH 15 seconds; stir until smooth.

Chocolate Chip Drizzle: Place 1/4 cup HERSHEY'S Semi-Sweet Chocolate Chips and 1/4 teaspoon shortening (do not use butter, margarine, spread or oil) in another small microwave-safe bowl. Microwave at HIGH (100%) 30 seconds to 1 minute; stir until chips are melted and mixture is smooth.

Chocolate Buttercream Cherry Candies

Josephine's Tea Cakes

1 package (18¼ ounces) pudding-in-the-mix yellow cake mix,
    plus ingredients to prepare mix
2 cups sifted powdered sugar, divided
8 tablespoons (1 stick) butter, melted, divided
8 teaspoons milk, divided
    Sugared Flowers and Fruits (recipe follows)

1. Prepare cake mix according to package directions. Bake in 10-inch square pan according to directions; allow extra time if necessary. Cool completely.

2. Set wire rack on large baking sheet. Remove cake from pan; place on cutting board. Cut cake into 1-inch squares; place squares on wire rack.

3. Combine 1 cup powdered sugar and 4 tablespoons butter in medium bowl; stir until blended. Add 4 teaspoons milk; stir until smooth. Working quickly, drizzle glaze over half of cake squares, allowing it to drip down sides. Repeat with remaining powdered sugar, butter and milk; drizzle over remaining cake squares.

4. Prepare Sugared Flowers and Fruits. Arrange on cake squares before serving.   *Makes 10 tea cakes*

Sugared Flowers and Fruits

    Assorted edible flowers
    Assorted small fruits (blueberries, raspberries, currants,
      kiwi pieces, kumquat slices)
1 pasteurized egg white
    Granulated sugar

Brush flower petals and fruit with egg white. Sprinkle generously with sugar; place on wire rack to dry. Use to decorate cakes.

Hint: You can make these crowd-pleasing tea cakes even if you don't have time to bake a cake! Just cut a frozen or store-bought pound cake into 1-inch squares and decorate as directed.

Josephine's Tea Cakes

English-Style Scones

3 eggs, divided
½ cup heavy cream
1½ teaspoons vanilla
2 cups all-purpose flour
2 teaspoons baking powder
¼ teaspoon salt
¼ cup (½ stick) cold butter
¼ cup finely chopped pitted dates
¼ cup golden raisins or currants
1 teaspoon water
6 tablespoons orange marmalade fruit spread
6 tablespoons whipped cream or crème fraîche

1. Preheat oven to 375°F. Beat 2 eggs with cream and vanilla; set aside.

2. Combine flour, baking powder and salt in medium bowl. Cut in butter with pastry blender or two knives until mixture resembles coarse crumbs. Stir in dates and raisins. Add cream mixture; mix just until dry ingredients are moistened. With floured hands, knead dough four times on lightly floured surface.

3. Place dough on greased cookie sheet; pat into 8-inch circle. With sharp wet knife, gently score dough into six wedges, cutting ¾ of the way into dough. Beat remaining egg with water; brush lightly over dough.

4. Bake 18 to 20 minutes or until golden brown. Cool 5 minutes on wire rack. Cut into wedges. Serve warm with marmalade and whipped cream.

Makes 6 scones

English-Style Scone

Ginger-Lemon Cheese Spread
with Pineapple-Peach Sauce

2 packages (8 ounces each) cream cheese, softened
1 cup sour cream
3 tablespoons packed brown sugar
1 tablespoon grated lemon peel
¾ teaspoon ground ginger
½ cup crushed pineapple, well drained
½ cup peach or apricot preserves
    Assorted crackers and fresh fruit

1. Line 3-cup decorative mold or bowl with plastic wrap.

2. Combine cream cheese and sour cream in large bowl; beat until creamy. (Do not overbeat.) Add brown sugar, lemon peel and ginger; stir until well blended.

3. Spoon cheese mixture into prepared mold. Cover with plastic wrap; refrigerate at least 8 hours or up to 2 days.

4. To complete recipe, combine pineapple and peach preserves in small bowl. Unmold cheese spread onto serving plate. Serve with sauce, crackers and fresh fruit.

Makes 8 servings

Variation: Press toasted chopped walnuts onto cheese spread and serve Pineapple-Peach Sauce alongside spread.

Ginger-Lemon Cheese Spread with Pineapple-Peach Sauce

Party Mints

1 (14-ounce) can EAGLE BRAND® Sweetened Condensed Milk
(NOT evaporated milk)
5½ cups confectioners' sugar
½ teaspoon peppermint extract
    Assorted colored granulated sugar or crystals

1. In medium mixing bowl, beat EAGLE BRAND® and half of confectioners' sugar until blended. Gradually add remaining confectioners' sugar and peppermint extract, beating until stiff.

2. Roll mixture into ½-inch balls; roll in desired sugar and place on parchment paper. Let stand 8 hours to set. Store covered at room temperature.   *Makes 3 dozen mints*

Tip: For smoothest texture, be sure to sift the confectioners' sugar before mixing. It will remove any lumps and make the mints extra creamy.

Variation: You many also dip uncoated mints in melted bittersweet chocolate for a different flavor.

Prep Time: 30 minutes
Stand Time: 8 hours

Dainty Tea Cookies

2½ cups all-purpose flour
½ teaspoon baking powder
⅛ teaspoon salt
1 cup (2 sticks) butter, softened
⅔ cup sugar
1 egg
1 teaspoon almond extract

1. Sift flour, baking powder and salt into medium bowl; set aside.

2. Beat remaining ingredients with electric mixer at medium speed until creamy. Gradually beat in flour mixture with mixer on low speed, mixing until just blended. Cover with plastic wrap; refrigerate at least 1 hour.

3. Preheat oven to 400°F. Lightly spray cookie sheets with nonstick cooking spray.

4. Fill cookie press with dough; press onto prepared cookie sheets, spacing 2 inches apart. Bake 10 to 12 minutes or until light golden brown. Let cookies stand on cookie sheet 1 minute. Remove cookies to wire racks; cool completely. *Makes about 4 dozen cookies*

Lemony Pound Cake

1 package (4-serving size) lemon-flavor gelatin
¾ cup boiling water
1 package DUNCAN HINES® Moist Deluxe® Classic Yellow
    Cake Mix
4 eggs
¾ cup vegetable oil
1 can (6 ounces) frozen lemonade concentrate, thawed
½ cup granulated sugar

1. Preheat oven to 350°F. Grease and flour 10-inch tube pan.

2. Dissolve gelatin in water in large mixing bowl; cool. Stir in cake mix, eggs and oil. Beat at medium speed with electric mixer for 2 minutes. Spoon into prepared pan. Bake 50 minutes or until toothpick inserted in center comes out clean. Mix lemonade concentrate and sugar in small bowl. Pour over hot cake; cool in pan 1 hour. Remove from pan. Cool completely.

Makes 12 to 16 servings

Serve Lemony Pound Cake with fresh or thawed frozen strawberries and whipped cream for a special dessert.

Vanilla Tea Time Cake

1 Butter Flavor CRISCO® Stick or 1 cup Butter Flavor
    CRISCO® all-vegetable shortening
2 cups sugar
6 eggs
1 package (12 ounces) vanilla wafers, ground to a coarse meal
½ cup milk
1 can (7½ ounces) sweetened flaked coconut
1 cup ground pecans

1. Heat oven to 300°F.

2. Beat 1 cup shortening and sugar in large bowl. Add eggs 1 at a time, beating well after each addition. Add vanilla wafers and milk; mix until blended. Add remaining ingredients; mix well.

3. Thoroughly spray 12-cup bundt pan with CRISCO® No-Stick Cooking Spray. Dust lightly with flour. Pour batter into pan; bake for 2 hours. Cool in pan on wire rack for 10 minutes. Run small sharp knife around edge of pan. Invert pan to release cake; cool completely on wire rack. *Makes 12 servings*

Turkey Canapes

8 JENNIE-O TURKEY STORE® Turkey Pastrami, turkey
    salami or turkey ham slices
32 buttery round crackers, wheat crackers or rye crackers
¾ cup (6 ounces) cream cheese with chives or herb-flavored
    cream cheese
1 small cucumber
    Fresh dill (optional)

Cut each slice of turkey into quarters; set aside. Spread each cracker with about 1 teaspoon cream cheese. Fold turkey quarters in half. Place turkey on cream cheese. Cut cucumber lengthwise in half; cut each half into ¼-inch slices. Top each cracker with cucumber slice and garnish with fresh dill, if desired. *Makes 32 servings*

Prep Time: 30 minutes

Vanilla Tea Time Cake

Chocolate Madeleines

1¼ cups all-purpose flour
1 cup sugar
⅛ teaspoon salt
¾ cup (1½ sticks) butter, melted (no substitutes)
⅓ cup HERSHEY'S Cocoa
3 eggs
2 egg yolks
½ teaspoon vanilla extract
Chocolate Frosting (recipe follows)

1. Heat oven to 350°F. Lightly grease indentations of madeleine mold pan (each shell is 3×2 inches).

2. Stir together flour, sugar and salt in medium saucepan. Combine melted butter and cocoa; stir into dry ingredients. In small bowl, lightly beat eggs, egg yolks and vanilla with fork until well blended; stir into chocolate mixture, blending well. Cook over very low heat, stirring constantly, until mixture is warm. *Do not simmer or boil.* Remove from heat. Fill each mold half full with batter. (Do not overfill).

3. Bake 8 to 10 minutes or until wooden toothpick inserted in center comes out clean. Invert onto wire rack; cool completely. Prepare Chocolate Frosting; frost flat sides of cookies. Press frosted sides together, forming shells. *Makes about 1½ dozen filled cookies*

Chocolate Frosting

1¼ cups powdered sugar
2 tablespoons HERSHEY'S Cocoa
2 tablespoons butter, softened (no substitutes)
2 to 2½ tablespoons milk
½ teaspoon vanilla extract

Stir together powdered sugar and cocoa in small bowl. In another small bowl, beat butter and ¼ cup of the cocoa mixture until fluffy. Gradually add remaining cocoa mixture alternately with milk, beating to spreading consistency. Stir in vanilla.

Chocolate Madeleines

Quick Pimiento Cheese Snacks

2 ounces cream cheese, softened
½ cup (2 ounces) shredded Cheddar cheese
1 jar (2 ounces) diced pimientos, drained
2 tablespoons finely chopped pecans
½ teaspoon hot pepper sauce
24 (¼-inch-thick) French bread slices or party bread slices

1. Preheat broiler.

2. Combine cream cheese and Cheddar cheese in small bowl; mix well. Stir in pimientos, pecans and hot pepper sauce.

3. Place bread slices on broiler pan or nonstick baking sheet. Broil 4 inches from heat 1 to 2 minutes or until lightly toasted on both sides.

4. Spread cheese mixture evenly onto bread slices. Broil 1 to 2 minutes or until cheese mixture is hot and bubbly. Transfer to serving plate; garnish, if desired.   *Makes 24 servings*

Tuna and Watercress Tea Sandwiches

1 (3-ounce) pouch of STARKIST Flavor Fresh Pouch® Albacore or Chunk Light Tuna
½ cup butter or margarine, softened
½ cup watercress leaves, firmly packed
2 tablespoons lemon juice
¼ teaspoon salt
⅛ teaspoon white pepper
24 slices thin white or wheat sandwich bread, crusts removed
Additional watercress, for garnish

In food processor bowl with metal blade, place tuna, butter, ½ cup watercress, lemon juice, salt and white pepper. Pulse on and off until watercress is finely chopped and mixture is blended. Spread tuna mixture on half the bread slices; top with remaining slices. Cut into squares or triangles. Serve or refrigerate up to 2 hours. Garnish with additional watercress.   *Makes 12 servings*

Note: Day-old bread is best for making tea sandwiches; it is easier to slice. Use a serrated knife.

Prep Time: 15 minutes

Quick Pimiento Cheese Snacks

White & Chocolate Covered Strawberries

2 cups (12-ounce package) HERSHEY'S Premier White Chips
2 tablespoons shortening (do not use butter, margarine, spread
    or oil)
1 cup HERSHEY'S Semi-Sweet Chocolate Chips
4 cups (2 pints) fresh strawberries, rinsed, patted dry and
    chilled

1. Cover tray with wax paper.

2. Place white chips and 1 tablespoon shortening in medium microwave-safe bowl. Microwave at HIGH (100%) 1 minute; stir until chips are melted and mixture is smooth. If necessary, microwave at HIGH an additional 30 seconds at a time, just until smooth when stirred.

3. Holding by top, dip ⅔ of each strawberry into white chip mixture; shake gently to remove excess. Place on prepared tray; refrigerate until coating is firm, at least 30 minutes.

4. Repeat microwave procedure with chocolate chips in clean microwave-safe bowl. Dip lower ⅓ of each berry into chocolate mixture. Refrigerate until firm. Cover; refrigerate leftover strawberries.

Makes 2 to 3 dozen berries

Hot Spiced Tea

4 cups freshly brewed tea
¼ cup honey
4 cinnamon sticks
4 whole cloves
4 lemon or orange slices (optional)

Combine tea, honey, cinnamon sticks and cloves in large saucepan; simmer 5 minutes. Serve hot. Garnish with lemon slices, if desired.

Makes 4 cups

Favorite recipe from **National Honey Board**

White & Chocolate Covered Strawberries (page 74)
and Mocha Truffles (page 89)

Elegant Berry Trifle

3 (3.4-ounce) packages vanilla pudding mix
1½ teaspoons almond extract, divided
½ cup white grape juice
1 (12-ounce) loaf pound cake, cut into ½-inch slices
½ cup SMUCKER'S® Red Raspberry Preserves
½ cup SMUCKER'S® Blackberry Preserves
1 cup whipping cream
1 tablespoon powdered sugar
1 teaspoon vanilla
8 crisp almond macaroon cookies, crushed, *or* ¼ cup
    toasted slivered almonds

Prepare pudding mixes according to package directions; cool. Blend in 1 teaspoon of the almond extract. Combine remaining ½ teaspoon extract with grape juice. Set aside.

Spread ¼ pound cake slices with raspberry preserves and ¼ with blackberry preserves; top each spread slice with unspread slice to form sandwiches. Cut sandwiches into ¾-inch-wide pieces. Reserve a few to garnish top of trifle; sprinkle remaining pieces with grape juice mixture.

To assemble trifle, spoon ⅓ pudding into 6-cup dessert dish or trifle bowl. Alternate raspberry and blackberry cake pieces in pattern on pudding, using half of pieces. Repeat procedure. Top with remaining pudding. Chill several hours.

Shortly before serving, whip cream with powdered sugar and vanilla until soft peaks form. Sprinkle crushed macaroons around edge of dish. Pipe rosettes or spoon dollops of whipped cream on top of trifle; garnish with reserved cake pieces. *Makes 10 to 12 servings*

Elegant Berry Trifle

Lemon Poppy Seed Tea Loaf

Tea Loaf

2½ cups all-purpose flour
¼ cup poppy seeds
1 tablespoon grated lemon peel
2 teaspoons baking powder
½ teaspoon baking soda
½ teaspoon salt
1 cup sugar
⅔ cup MOTT'S® Natural Apple Sauce
1 whole egg
2 egg whites, lightly beaten
2 tablespoons vegetable oil
1 teaspoon vanilla extract
⅓ cup skim milk

Lemon Syrup

¼ cup sugar
¼ cup lemon juice

1. Preheat oven to 350°F. Spray 9×5-inch loaf pan with nonstick cooking spray.

2. To prepare Tea Loaf, in large bowl, combine flour, poppy seeds, lemon peel, baking powder, baking soda and salt.

3. In medium bowl, combine 1 cup sugar, apple sauce, whole egg, egg whites, oil and vanilla.

4. Stir apple sauce mixture into flour mixture alternately with milk. Mix until thoroughly moistened. Spread batter into prepared pan.

5. Bake 40 to 45 minutes or until toothpick inserted in center comes out clean. Cool in pan 10 minutes. Invert onto wire rack; turn right side up.

6. To prepare Lemon Syrup, in small saucepan, combine ¼ cup sugar and lemon juice. Cook, stirring frequently, until sugar dissolves. Cool slightly.

7. Pierce top of loaf in several places with metal skewer. Brush lemon syrup over loaf. Let stand until cool. Cut into 16 slices.

Makes 16 servings

Lemon Poppy Seed Tea Loaf

Shrimp Toast

½ pound raw shrimp, peeled and deveined
2 tablespoons chopped green onion
2 tablespoons finely chopped water chestnuts
2 tablespoons soy sauce
1 teaspoon dark sesame oil
1 egg white, lightly beaten
6 slices white sandwich bread, crusts removed
    Red and yellow bell pepper strips, for garnish

1. Finely chop shrimp. If using food processor, process with on/off pulses, about 10 times or until shrimp are finely chopped.

2. Combine shrimp, onion, water chestnuts, soy sauce and sesame oil in medium bowl; mix well. Stir in egg white; mix well.*

3. Toast bread lightly on both sides. Cut diagonally into quarters. Spread shrimp mixture evenly over toast to edges.

4. Place toast on foil-lined baking sheet or broiler pan. Broil 6 inches from heat 4 minutes or until lightly browned. Garnish with peppers.

Makes 2 dozen appetizers

The filling may be made ahead to this point. Cover and refrigerate filling up to 24 hours. Proceed as directed in step 3.

BelGioioso® Gorgonzola Spread

2 cups BELGIOIOSO® Mascarpone
½ cup BELGIOIOSO® Gorgonzola
2 tablespoons chopped fresh basil
½ cup chopped walnuts
    Sliced apples and pears

In small bowl, combine BelGioioso Mascarpone, BelGioioso Gorgonzola and basil. Mix to blend well. Transfer mixture to serving bowl; cover and refrigerate 2 hours. Before serving, sprinkle with walnuts and arrange sliced apples and pears around bowl.

Makes 8 servings

Tip: This spread can also be served with fresh vegetables, crackers, Melba toast or bread.

Shrimp Toast

Lemon Curd Tartlets
with Fresh Raspberries

3 egg yolks
½ cup sugar
⅓ cup fresh lemon juice
1 teaspoon grated lemon peel
6 tablespoons I CAN'T BELIEVE IT'S NOT BUTTER!®
    Spread, cut in pieces
24 frozen mini phyllo dough shells, thawed
½ cup whipped cream or non-dairy whipped topping
24 fresh raspberries

In top of double boiler, with wire whisk, beat egg yolks, sugar, lemon juice and lemon peel until blended. Stir in I Can't Believe It's Not Butter!® Spread. Cook over medium heat, stirring frequently, 10 minutes or until mixture thickens and reaches 160°F.

Turn into large bowl and cover with plastic wrap, pressing wrap on surface of lemon curd; refrigerate to chill completely, about 2 hours.

To serve, evenly fill shells with lemon curd. Garnish with whipped cream and raspberries.   *Makes about 2 dozen tartlets*

Smoked Salmon Lavash

4 ounces cream cheese, softened
1 tablespoon lemon juice
¼ teaspoon prepared horseradish
4 small lavash (about 5 inches)
4 ounces sliced smoked salmon
½ red onion, thinly sliced
2 tablespoons capers, drained

Combine cream cheese, lemon juice and horseradish in small bowl. Spread carefully over lavash. Top with salmon, onion and capers.
                                        Makes 4 servings

Lemon Curd Tartlets with Fresh Raspberries

Mini Lemon Sandwich Cookies

Cookies
  2 cups all-purpose flour
  1 cup (2 sticks) butter, softened
  ⅓ cup whipping cream
  ¼ cup granulated sugar
  1 teaspoon lemon peel
  ⅛ teaspoon lemon extract
    Additional granulated sugar

Filling
  ¾ cup powdered sugar
  ¼ cup (½ stick) butter, softened
  1 to 3 teaspoons lemon juice
  1 teaspoon vanilla
    Food coloring (optional)

1. For cookies, combine flour, 1 cup butter, whipping cream, ¼ cup granulated sugar, lemon peel and lemon extract in medium bowl. Beat 2 to 3 minutes, scraping bowl often, until well blended. Divide dough into thirds. Wrap each portion in waxed paper; refrigerate until firm.

2. Preheat oven to 375°F. Roll each portion of dough to ⅛-inch thickness on well-floured surface. Cut dough with 1½-inch round cookie cutter. Dip both sides of each cookie in additional granulated sugar. Place 1 inch apart on ungreased cookie sheets. Pierce with fork. Bake 6 to 9 minutes or until slightly puffed but not brown. Cool 1 minute on cookie sheets; remove to wire racks to cool completely.

3. For filling, combine powdered sugar, ¼ cup butter, lemon juice and vanilla in small bowl. Beat 1 to 2 minutes, scraping bowl often, until smooth. Tint with food coloring, if desired. Spread ½ teaspoon filling each on bottoms of half the cookies; top with remaining cookies.

Makes 4½ dozen sandwich cookies

Mini Lemon Sandwich Cookies

Chutney Cheese Spread

2 packages (8 ounces each) cream cheese, softened
1 cup (4 ounces) shredded Cheddar cheese
½ cup mango chutney
¼ cup thinly sliced green onions with tops
3 tablespoons dark raisins, chopped
2 cloves garlic, minced
1 to 1½ teaspoons curry powder
¾ teaspoon ground coriander
½ to ¾ teaspoon ground ginger
1 tablespoon chopped dry roasted peanuts

1. Place cream cheese and Cheddar cheese in food processor or blender; process until smooth. Stir in chutney, green onions, raisins, garlic, curry powder, coriander and ginger. Cover; refrigerate 2 to 3 hours.

2. Top spread with peanuts. Serve with additional green onions and melba toast, if desired.   *Makes 20 (2-tablespoon) servings*

Tip: The spread can also be garnished with one tablespoon toasted coconut to provide a slightly sweeter flavor.

Cracker Bites

1 pound JENNIE-O TURKEY STORE® Deli Premium
    Seasoned Brown Sugar Roasted Turkey Breast,
    thinly shaved
1 (7-ounce) package Carr's® Water Crackers, 3 inch size
6 ounces pineapple preserves

Lay crackers on flat surface. Mound with ¾ ounce to 1 ounce of JENNIE-O TURKEY STORE® Premium Seasoned Brown Sugar Turkey Breast. Dollop with teaspoon of preserves. Place on appetizer platter surrounded by fresh pineapple spears.

Variations: Any variety of JENNIE-O TURKEY STORE® turkey breast can be used in this recipe. Any thick preserve could be used instead of pineapple. Substitute dark cherry, apricot or peach preserves.

Prep Time: 15 minutes

Chutney Cheese Spread

Orange Apricot Tea Bread

¾ cup water
6 LIPTON® Soothing Moments® Orange & Spice Flavored
    Tea Bags
½ cup chopped dried apricots
2½ cups all-purpose flour
1¼ cups sugar
  2 teaspoons baking powder
  1 teaspoon salt
⅓ cup I CAN'T BELIEVE IT'S NOT BUTTER!®
    Spread-stick, softened
  2 large eggs
  1 container (8 ounces) vanilla yogurt

Preheat oven to 350°F. Spray 9×5-inch loaf pan with nonstick cooking spray; set aside.

In 1-quart saucepan, bring water to a boil. Remove from heat and add orange & spice flavored tea bags and apricots; cover and steep 5 minutes. Remove tea bags and squeeze; cool.

In large bowl, mix flour, sugar, baking powder and salt. With electric mixer, cut in butter until mixture is size of small peas. Add eggs beaten with cool tea and yogurt; stir just until flour is moistened. Turn into prepared pan. Bake 1 hour 5 minutes or until toothpick inserted into center comes out clean. Cool 10 minutes on wire rack; remove from pan and cool completely. *Makes 1 loaf*

Mocha Truffles

2 cups (11½ ounces) milk chocolate chips
½ cup whipping cream
2 teaspoons instant coffee granules
2 tablespoons coffee-flavored liqueur
⅔ cup vanilla wafer crumbs (about 15 wafers)

1. Melt chips with whipping cream and coffee granules in heavy, medium saucepan over low heat, stirring occasionally. Whisk in liqueur until blended. Pour into pie pan. Refrigerate until mixture is fudgy, but soft, about 2 hours.

2. Shape about 1 tablespoon of mixture into 1¼-inch ball. Place ball on waxed paper. Repeat with remaining mixture.

3. Place crumbs in shallow bowl.

4. Roll balls in crumbs; place in petit four or candy cases. (If coating mixture won't stick because truffle has set, roll between palms until outside is soft.)

5. Truffles can be refrigerated 2 to 3 days or frozen several weeks.

Makes about 30 truffles

Note: To enjoy the full flavor of truffles, bring to room temperature before serving.

For all royal events, treat your guests to truffles—rich and elegant chocolate French candies. Make these ahead of time and freeze. You'll be ready with an exquisite and lavish sweet for any celebration.

Sweet Delights

Chocolate Raspberry Dessert

1 cup all-purpose flour
1 cup sugar
½ cup (1 stick) butter or margarine, softened
¼ teaspoon baking powder
4 eggs
1½ cups (16-ounce can) HERSHEY'S Syrup
    Raspberry Cream Center (recipe follows)
    Chocolate Glaze (recipe follows)

1. Heat oven to 350°F. Grease 13×9×2-inch baking pan.

2. Combine flour, sugar, butter, baking powder and eggs in large bowl; beat until smooth. Add syrup; blend thoroughly. Pour batter into prepared pan.

3. Bake 25 to 30 minutes or until wooden pick inserted in center comes out clean. Cool completely in pan on wire rack. Spread Raspberry Cream Center on cake. Cover; refrigerate. Pour Chocolate Glaze over chilled dessert. Cover; refrigerate at least 1 hour before serving. Cover; refrigerate leftover dessert. *Makes about 12 servings*

Raspberry Cream Center: Combine 2 cups powdered sugar, ½ cup (1 stick) softened butter or margarine and 2 tablespoons raspberry-flavored liqueur* in small bowl; beat until smooth. (A few drops red food coloring may be added, if desired.)

¼ cup raspberry preserves and 1 teaspoon water may be substituted for the raspberry-flavored liqueur.

Chocolate Glaze: Melt 6 tablespoons butter or margarine and 1 cup HERSHEY'S Semi-Sweet Chocolate Chips in small saucepan over very low heat. Remove from heat; stir until smooth. Cool slightly.

Chocolate Raspberry Dessert

Cheesecake Sensation

¼ cup graham cracker crumbs
1½ tablespoons unflavored gelatin
4 (8-ounce) packages cream cheese, softened
4 eggs
1¾ cups sugar
2 tablespoons lemon juice
2 tablespoons grated lemon peel
1 teaspoon vanilla
½ cup SMUCKER'S® Natural Apricot Syrup
½ cup SMUCKER'S® Strawberry Preserves

Preheat oven to 325°F.

Grease inside of straight-sided, 8×3-inch casserole or soufflé dish. Sprinkle with graham cracker crumbs and shake around bottom and sides. Set aside.

Sprinkle gelatin over ¼ cup cold water. Let sit 5 minutes. Heat in microwave until gelatin is melted, clear and completely dissolved. Set aside.

Combine cream cheese, eggs, sugar, lemon juice, lemon peel and vanilla; beat at low speed and, as ingredients blend, increase speed to high, scraping bowl several times. Continue beating until thoroughly blended and smooth. Stir in gelatin. Pour batter into prepared dish; shake gently to level mixture. Set dish inside slightly wider pan; add boiling water to larger pan to a depth of about ½-inch.

Bake for 1½ to 2 hours or until set. Turn off oven and let cake sit in oven 20 minutes longer. Place cake dish on wire rack. Cool about 2 hours or until room temperature.

Invert plate over the cheesecake and carefully turn upside down so cake comes out crumb side up. Spoon SMUCKER'S® syrup over cake and SMUCKER'S® preserves in a narrow ring around outer rim of cake. *Makes 12 to 14 servings*

Cheesecake Sensation

Individual Chocolate Coconut Cheesecakes

  1 cup chocolate cookie crumbs
  ¼ cup (½ stick) butter, melted
  2 packages (8 ounces each) cream cheese, softened
  ⅓ cup sugar
  2 eggs
  1 teaspoon vanilla
  ¼ teaspoon coconut extract (optional)
  ½ cup flaked coconut
  ½ cup semisweet chocolate chips
  1 teaspoon shortening

1. Preheat oven to 325°F. Line twelve 2½-inch muffin pan cups with foil or paper baking cups.

2. Combine cookie crumbs and butter in small bowl. Press onto bottoms of baking cups.

3. Combine cream cheese and sugar in large bowl. Beat 2 minutes at medium speed of electric mixer until well blended. Add eggs, vanilla and coconut extract, if desired. Beat just until blended. Stir in coconut.

4. Carefully spoon about ¼ cup cream cheese mixture into each baking cup. Bake 18 to 22 minutes or until nearly set. Cool 30 minutes in pan on wire rack. Remove from pan. Peel away baking cups.

5. Combine chocolate chips and shortening in small saucepan. Cook and stir over low heat until chocolate chips are melted. Drizzle over tops of cheesecakes. Let stand 20 minutes. Cover; refrigerate until ready to serve. *Makes 12 servings*

Sweet Delights

Individual Chocolate Coconut Cheesecakes

Dreamy Orange Cream Puffs

Cream Puffs (recipe follows)
¾ cup granulated sugar
3 tablespoons cornstarch
1½ cups orange juice
3 egg yolks, beaten
1 cup plain yogurt
2 tablespoons butter
½ teaspoon almond extract
1 can (11 ounces) mandarin oranges, drained
Powdered sugar

1. Prepare Cream Puffs.

2. Combine sugar, cornstarch and orange juice in medium saucepan. Cook over medium heat until bubbly, stirring often. Cook 2 minutes; remove from heat. Gradually stir half of hot mixture into egg yolks. Return to saucepan; bring to a boil over medium-high heat. Reduce heat to low. Cook 2 minutes; remove from heat. Stir in yogurt, butter and extract.

3. To serve, spoon filling into bottoms of cream puffs. Pile orange sections on top of filling. Add cream puff tops. Lightly sift powdered sugar over tops. *Makes 6 servings*

Cream Puffs

1 cup water
½ cup (1 stick) butter
1 cup all-purpose flour
½ teaspoon salt
4 eggs

1. Preheat oven to 400°F. Grease baking sheet.

2. Combine water and butter in medium saucepan; bring to a boil, stirring until butter melts. Add flour and salt, all at once, stirring vigorously. Cook and stir until mixture forms a ball that does not separate. Remove from heat and cool 10 minutes. Add eggs, 1 at a time, beating after each addition until mixture is smooth.

3. Drop heaping tablespoons of batter into 6 mounds, 3 inches apart, onto prepared baking sheet. Bake about 35 minutes or until golden brown and puffy. Cool slightly. Cut off tops and remove soft dough inside. Cool completely on wire rack. *Makes 6 cream puffs*

Dreamy Orange Cream Puffs

Berry-Berry Brownie Torte

½ cup all-purpose flour
¼ teaspoon baking soda
¼ teaspoon salt
1 cup HERSHEY'S Raspberry Chips or HERSHEY'S
    Semi-Sweet Chocolate Chips
½ cup (1 stick) butter or margarine
1¼ cups sugar, divided
 2 eggs
 1 teaspoon vanilla extract
⅓ cup HERSHEY'S Dutch Processed Cocoa
½ cup whipping cream
¾ cup fresh blackberries, rinsed and patted dry
¾ cup fresh raspberries, rinsed and patted dry

1. Heat oven to 350°F. Line with wax paper, then grease 9-inch round baking pan. Stir together flour, baking soda and salt. Stir in raspberry chips.

2. Melt butter in medium saucepan over low heat. Remove from heat. Stir in 1 cup sugar, eggs and vanilla. Add cocoa, blending well. Stir in flour mixture. Spread mixture in prepared pan.

3. Bake 20 to 25 minutes or until wooden pick inserted in center comes out slightly sticky. Cool in pan on wire rack 15 minutes. Invert onto wire rack; remove wax paper. Turn right side up; cool completely.

4. Beat whipping cream and remaining ¼ cup sugar until sugar is dissolved and stiff peaks form. Spread over top of brownie. Top with berries. Refrigerate until serving time.   *Makes 8 to 10 servings*

Berry-Berry Brownie Torte

Frozen Lemon Squares

1¼ cups graham cracker crumbs
¼ cup sugar
¼ cup (½ stick) butter or margarine, melted
1 (14-ounce) can EAGLE BRAND® Sweetened Condensed Milk
    (NOT evaporated milk)
3 egg yolks
½ cup lemon juice from concentrate
    Yellow food coloring (optional)
    Whipped cream or non-dairy whipped topping

1. Preheat oven to 325°F. In small mixing bowl, combine crumbs, sugar and butter; press firmly on bottom of 8- or 9-inch square pan.

2. In small mixing bowl, beat EAGLE BRAND,® egg yolks, lemon juice and food coloring (optional). Pour into crust.

3. Bake 30 minutes. Cool completely. Top with whipped cream. Freeze 4 hours or until firm. Let stand 10 minutes before serving. Garnish as desired. Freeze leftovers.   *Makes 6 to 9 servings*

Famous Tiramisu Dessert Recipe

3 large pasteurized eggs, separating whites and yolks
1 cup espresso or strong coffee
½ cup sugar
2 tablespoons cognac or brandy
8 ounces BELGIOIOSO® Mascarpone
20 ladyfingers (toasted)
⅛ cup cocoa

Combine 3 egg yolks, 1 tablespoon espresso, sugar, and cognac into large mixing bowl. Beat 2 to 3 minutes. Add BelGioioso Mascarpone and beat 3 to 5 minutes until consistency is smooth.

In another bowl, combine 3 egg whites and a pinch of sugar. Beat until mixture forms stiff peaks. Gently fold into Mascarpone mixture.

Pour rest of espresso into flat dish, dip one side of each ladyfinger, and layer on bottom of serving dish. Spread ½ of Mascarpone mixture and sprinkle with cocoa. Layer ladyfingers and finish with a Mascarpone layer and cocoa. Refrigerate at least 1 hour before serving.

Makes 6 servings

Frozen Lemon Square

Easy Chocoberry Cream Dessert

2 packages (3 ounces *each*) ladyfingers, split
1 package (10 ounces) frozen strawberries in syrup, thawed
    and drained
2 envelopes unflavored gelatin
2 cups milk, divided
1 cup sugar
⅓ cup HERSHEY'S Cocoa or HERSHEY'S Dutch Processed
    Cocoa
¼ cup (½ stick) butter or margarine
1 teaspoon vanilla extract
2 cups frozen non-dairy whipped topping, thawed
    Additional whipped topping (optional)
    Fresh strawberries (optional)
    Mint leaves (optional)

1. Place ladyfingers, cut side in, on bottom and around sides of 9-inch springform pan.

2. Purée strawberries in food processor. Sprinkle gelatin over 1 cup milk in medium saucepan; let stand 2 minutes to soften. Add sugar, cocoa and butter. Cook over medium heat, stirring constantly, until mixture is hot and gelatin is completely dissolved. Remove from heat; stir in remaining 1 cup milk, vanilla and puréed strawberries. Refrigerate until mixture begins to thicken.

3. Fold 2 cups whipped topping into gelatin mixture. Pour mixture into prepared pan. Cover; refrigerate until mixture is firm. Just before serving, remove side of pan. Garnish with additional whipped topping, fresh strawberries and mint, if desired. Cover; refrigerate leftover dessert. *Makes 10 to 12 servings*

Easy Chocoberry Cream Dessert

Chocolate Dream Cups

1 cup HERSHEY'S Semi-Sweet Chocolate Chips
1 teaspoon shortening (do not use butter, margarine, spread
   or oil)
Chocolate Filling or Raspberry Filling (recipes follow)

1. Line 6 muffin cups (2½ inches in diameter) with paper cup liners.

2. Place chocolate chips and shortening in small microwave-safe bowl. Microwave at HIGH (100%) 1 minute; stir. If necessary, microwave at HIGH 30 seconds or until chips are melted and mixture is smooth when stirred.

3. Coat inside pleated surface and bottoms of cup liners thickly and evenly with melted chocolate using a soft-bristled pastry brush. Refrigerate coated cups 10 minutes or until set; recoat any thin spots with melted chocolate. (If necessary, chocolate can be reheated on HIGH for a few seconds.) Refrigerate cups until very firm, 2 hours or overnight. Carefully peel paper from each chocolate cup. Cover; refrigerate until ready to use.

4. Prepare either Chocolate or Raspberry Filling. Spoon or pipe into chocolate cups; refrigerate until set. Garnish as desired.

Makes 6 dessert cups

Chocolate Filling

1 teaspoon unflavored gelatin
1 tablespoon cold water
2 tablespoons boiling water
½ cup sugar
¼ cup HERSHEY'S Cocoa
1 cup (8 ounces) cold whipping cream
1 teaspoon vanilla extract

1. Sprinkle gelatin over cold water in small bowl; let stand 1 minute to soften. Add boiling water; stir until gelatin is completely dissolved and mixture is clear. Cool slightly.

2. Stir together sugar and cocoa in another small bowl; add whipping cream and vanilla. Beat on medium speed until stiff, scraping bottom of bowl occasionally. Pour in gelatin mixture; beat until well blended.

Add even more great recipes to your collection!

This $3.99 voucher entitles you to a

FREE MAGAZINE

as our way of saying

thank you

for your purchase!

Just send in this card to register and we'll send you the next issue of EASY HOME COOKING Magazine FREE!

- More than 50 mouthwatering recipes featuring your favorite brand name foods.
- Beautiful color photos of finished recipes, plus helpful Cook's Notes and easy-to-follow cooking instructions.

Name _____

Address _____

City/State/ZIP _____

Canadian residents, please enclose $1.50 (U.S. funds) for postage. This offer is not available outside North America. Please allow 4-6 weeks for delivery of first issue.

S69DGD

BUSINESS REPLY MAIL
FIRST-CLASS MAIL   PERMIT NO. 24   MT. MORRIS, IL

POSTAGE WILL BE PAID BY ADDRESSEE

EASY HOME COOKING
PO BOX 520
MT MORRIS IL 61054-7451

Raspberry Filling

1 package (10 ounces) frozen red raspberries, thawed
1 teaspoon unflavored gelatin
1 tablespoon cold water
2 tablespoons boiling water
1 cup (8 ounces) cold whipping cream
¼ cup powdered sugar
½ teaspoon vanilla extract
3 to 4 drops red food coloring

1. Drain raspberries; press berries through sieve to remove seeds. Discard seeds.

2. Sprinkle gelatin over cold water in small bowl; let stand 1 minute to soften. Add boiling water; stir until gelatin is completely dissolved and mixture is clear. Cool slightly.

3. Beat whipping cream and sugar in another small bowl until soft peaks form; pour in gelatin mixture and beat until stiff. Carefully fold in raspberry purée and food coloring; refrigerate 20 minutes.

Chocolate Dream Cups

Pumpkin Pecan Rum Cake

¾ cup chopped pecans
3 cups all-purpose flour
2 tablespoons pumpkin pie spice
2 teaspoons baking soda
1 teaspoon salt
1 cup (2 sticks) butter or margarine, softened
1 cup packed brown sugar
1 cup granulated sugar
4 large eggs
1 can (15 ounces) LIBBY'S® 100% Pure Pumpkin
1 teaspoon vanilla extract
   Rum Butter Glaze (recipe follows)

PREHEAT oven to 325°F. Grease 12-cup Bundt pan. Sprinkle nuts over bottom.

COMBINE flour, pumpkin pie spice, baking soda and salt in medium bowl. Beat butter, brown sugar and granulated sugar in large mixer bowl until light and fluffy. Add eggs; beat well. Add pumpkin and vanilla extract; beat well. Add flour mixture to pumpkin mixture, ⅓ at a time, mixing well after each addition. Spoon batter into prepared pan.

BAKE for 60 to 70 minutes or until wooden pick comes out clean. Cool 10 minutes. Make holes in cake with long pick; pour *half* of glaze over cake. Let stand 5 minutes and invert onto plate. Make holes in top of cake; pour *remaining* glaze over cake. Cool. Garnish as desired.

Makes 24 servings

Rum Butter Glaze: MELT ¼ cup butter or margarine in small saucepan; stir in ½ cup granulated sugar and 2 tablespoons water. Bring to a boil. Remove from heat; stir in 2 to 3 tablespoons dark rum or 1 teaspoon rum extract.

Pumpkin Pecan Rum Cake

Chocolate Chiffon Pie

2 (1-ounce) squares unsweetened chocolate, chopped
1 (14-ounce) can EAGLE BRAND® Sweetened Condensed Milk
 (NOT evaporated milk)
1 envelope unflavored gelatin
⅓ cup water
½ teaspoon vanilla extract
1 cup (½ pint) whipping cream, whipped
1 (6-ounce) chocolate or graham cracker crumb pie crust
 Additional whipped cream

1. In heavy saucepan over low heat, melt chocolate with EAGLE BRAND.® Remove from heat.

2. Meanwhile, in small saucepan, sprinkle gelatin over water; let stand 1 minute. Over low heat, stir until gelatin dissolves.

3. Stir gelatin into chocolate mixture. Add vanilla. Cool to room temperature. Fold in whipped cream. Spread into crust.

4. Chill 3 hours or until set. Garnish with additional whipped cream. Store covered in refrigerator.

Makes 1 pie

Prep Time: 20 minutes
Chill Time: 3 hours

Tasty Tip

Chocolate curls are a beautiful finishing touch for the top of a delicious dessert. To make decorative chocolate curls, bring a bar of semisweet or milk chocolate to room temperature. Run a clean vegetable peeler along the surface of the chocolate to create curls.

Chocolate Chiffon Pie

Strawberry Charlotte

4 fresh strawberries, sliced
⅔ cup plus 3 tablespoons sugar, divided
1 teaspoon unflavored gelatin
2½ cups milk
1 package (6-serving size) vanilla pudding mix
1 package (16 ounces) frozen unsweetened strawberries, thawed
  and undrained
3 cups thawed frozen nondairy whipped topping, divided
⅔ cup chopped fresh strawberries or whole fresh blueberries
1 package (7 ounces) dry Champagne biscuits (4-inch-long
  ladyfinger-like biscuits)
Additional fresh strawberries or blueberries

1. Line bottom and side of 5-cup soufflé dish with heavy duty plastic wrap. Arrange sliced strawberries in bottom of prepared dish.

2. Bring ⅔ cup sugar and ⅔ cup water to a boil in small saucepan, stirring constantly, until sugar melts. Remove from heat; cool.

3. Combine gelatin and 1 tablespoon water in small bowl. Combine milk and pudding mix in large saucepan. Cook and stir over medium heat until mixture comes to a boil. Remove from heat. Add gelatin to pudding mixture; stir until gelatin dissolves. Transfer mixture to large bowl; cool slightly.

4. Place frozen strawberries in food processor or blender; process until smooth. Stir ½ cup strawberry purée into pudding mixture; let stand 15 to 20 minutes or until cool but not set, stirring occasionally. Gently fold 2½ cups whipped topping and chopped strawberries into pudding mixture.

5. Trim about 15 biscuits to 3-inch lengths. Dip into sugar mixture, allowing excess to drip back into saucepan. Arrange biscuits around side of prepared dish, sides touching and rounded ends pointing up. Spoon pudding mixture into prepared dish. Dip remaining biscuits in sugar mixture, allowing excess to drip back into saucepan; arrange on top of pudding mixture. Cover and refrigerate overnight.

6. Stir remaining 3 tablespoons sugar into remaining strawberry purée; cover and refrigerate overnight. To complete recipe, unmold charlotte onto serving platter; remove plastic wrap. Serve with strawberry purée and remaining ½ cup whipped topping.

Makes 6 servings

Sweet Delights

Strawberry Charlotte

Passionate Profiteroles

Vanilla Custard Filling (page 113)
⅔ cup water
7 tablespoons plus 2 teaspoons I CAN'T BELIEVE IT'S NOT
    BUTTER!® Spread, divided
1 tablespoon sugar
¼ teaspoon salt
¾ cup all-purpose flour
4 large eggs
1 square (1 ounce) semi-sweet chocolate
    Toasted sliced almonds (optional)

Prepare Vanilla Custard Filling. Preheat oven to 400°F. Lightly grease
baking sheet; set aside.

In 2½-quart saucepan, bring water, 7 tablespoons I Can't Believe It's
Not Butter!® Spread, sugar and salt to a boil over high heat. Remove
from heat and immediately stir in flour. Cook flour mixture over
medium heat, stirring constantly with wooden spoon 5 minutes or until
film forms on bottom of pan. Remove from heat; stir in eggs, one at a
time, beating well after each addition. Immediately drop by heaping
tablespoonfuls onto prepared baking sheet. Place baking sheet on
middle rack in oven.

Bake 20 minutes. Decrease oven temperature to 350°F and bake an
additional 20 minutes. Turn off oven without opening door and let
profiteroles stand in oven 10 minutes. Cool completely on wire rack.
To fill, slice off top ⅓ of profiteroles and set aside. Fill with Vanilla
Custard Filling. Replace profiterole tops.

In small microwave-safe bowl, microwave chocolate and remaining
2 teaspoons I Can't Believe It's Not Butter! Spread at HIGH (Full
Power) 30 seconds or until chocolate is melted; stir until smooth.
Drizzle chocolate mixture over profiteroles, then sprinkle, if desired,
with toasted sliced almonds.   *Makes 16 servings*

Vanilla Custard Filling

1 package (3.4 ounces) instant vanilla pudding
1 cup milk
3 to 4 tablespoons hazelnut, coffee, almond, orange or cherry
    liqueur (optional)
½ teaspoon vanilla extract
2 cups whipped cream or non-dairy whipped topping

In medium bowl, with wire whisk, blend pudding mix, milk, liqueur and vanilla. Fold in whipped cream. Cover with plastic wrap and refrigerate 1 hour or until set.

Passionate Profiteroles

Mandarin Orange Tea Cake

1 package (16 ounces) pound cake mix
½ cup plus 2 tablespoons orange juice, divided
2 eggs
¼ cup milk
1 can (15 ounces) mandarin orange segments in light syrup,
    drained
¾ cup powdered sugar
    Grated peel of 1 orange

1. Preheat oven to 350°F. Grease 9-inch Bundt pan.

2. Beat cake mix, ½ cup orange juice, eggs and milk in large
bowl 2 minutes on medium speed of electric mixer or until light and
fluffy. Fold in orange segments; pour batter into prepared pan.

3. Bake 45 minutes or until golden brown and toothpick inserted near
center comes out clean. Cool in pan 15 minutes on wire rack. Invert
cake onto wire rack; cool completely.

4. For glaze, combine sugar, peel and remaining 2 tablespoons orange
juice in small bowl; beat until smooth. Drizzle glaze over cake. Allow
glaze to set about 5 minutes before serving.   ***Makes 16 servings***

Tasty Tip

*A Bundt pan allows the cook to make a beautiful tall cake without the
worry of layers. The hollow center helps the cake bake evenly on all sides.
Always be sure to thoroughly grease the nooks and crannies in the Bundt
pan so you can unmold the cake easily. And, cooling the cake in the pan
is another important step to successfully unmold the cake.*

Mandarin Orange Tea Cake

Holiday Fanfare

Cherry Eggnog Quick Bread

2½ cups all-purpose flour
¾ cup sugar
1 tablespoon baking powder
½ teaspoon ground nutmeg
1¼ cups prepared dairy eggnog or half-and-half
6 tablespoons butter, melted and cooled
2 eggs, lightly beaten
1 teaspoon vanilla
½ cup chopped pecans
½ cup coarsely chopped candied red cherries

1. Preheat oven to 350°F. Grease three 5½×3-inch mini-loaf pans.

2. Combine flour, sugar, baking powder and nutmeg in large bowl. Stir eggnog, melted butter, eggs and vanilla in medium bowl until well blended. Add eggnog mixture to flour mixture. Mix just until all ingredients are moistened. Stir in pecans and cherries. Spoon into prepared pans.

3. Bake 35 to 40 minutes or until wooden toothpick inserted into centers comes out clean. Cool in pans 15 minutes. Remove from pans and cool completely on wire rack. Store tightly wrapped in plastic wrap at room temperature. *Makes 3 mini loaves*

Cherry Eggnog Quick Bread

Kahlúa® Marbled Pumpkin Cheesecake

¾ cup gingersnap crumbs
¾ cup graham cracker crumbs
¼ cup powdered sugar
¼ cup (4 tablespoons) melted unsalted butter
2 (8-ounce) packages cream cheese, softened
1 cup granulated sugar
4 eggs
1 (1-pound) can pumpkin
½ teaspoon ground cinnamon
¼ teaspoon ground ginger
¼ teaspoon ground nutmeg
½ cup KAHLÚA® Liqueur

Heat oven to 350°F. In bowl, combine gingersnap and graham cracker crumbs with powdered sugar and butter. Toss to combine. Press evenly onto bottom of 8-inch springform pan. Bake 5 minutes. Cool.

In mixer bowl, beat cream cheese until smooth. Gradually add granulated sugar and beat until light. Add eggs, one at a time, beating well after each addition. Transfer 1 cup mixture to separate bowl and blend in pumpkin, cinnamon, ginger, nutmeg and Kahlúa®. Pour half of pumpkin mixture into prepared crust. Top with half of cream cheese mixture. Repeat layers using remaining pumpkin and cream cheese mixtures. Using table knife, cut through layers with uplifting motion in four to five places to create marbled effect. Place on baking sheet and bake at 350°F for 45 minutes. Without opening oven door, let cake stand in turned-off oven 1 hour. Remove from oven and cool, then chill. Remove from pan. *Makes about 12 servings*

Kahlúa® Marbled Pumpkin Cheesecake

Holiday Peppermint Bark

2 cups (12-ounce package) NESTLÉ® TOLL HOUSE®
    Premier White Morsels
24 hard peppermint candies, unwrapped

LINE baking sheet with wax paper.

MICROWAVE morsels in medium, uncovered, microwave-safe bowl on MEDIUM-HIGH (70%) power for 1 minute. STIR. Morsels may retain some of their original shape. If necessary, microwave at additional 10- to 15-second intervals, stirring just until morsels are melted.

PLACE peppermint candies in *heavy-duty* resealable plastic food storage bag. Crush candies using rolling pin or other heavy object. While holding strainer over melted morsels, pour crushed candy into strainer. Shake to release all small candy pieces; reserve larger candy pieces. Stir morsel-peppermint mixture.

SPREAD mixture to desired thickness on prepared baking sheet. Sprinkle with reserved candy pieces; press in lightly. Let stand for about 1 hour or until firm. Break into pieces. Store in airtight container at room temperature.   *Makes about 1 pound candy*

Quick Hot Spiced Cider

8 cups MOTT'S® Apple Juice
2 tablespoons brown sugar
1 teaspoon whole allspice
1 teaspoon whole cloves
8 cinnamon sticks

Combine apple juice, brown sugar, allspice and cloves in large pot. Bring to boil, then simmer 15 minutes. Remove cloves and allspice. Add cinnamon stick to each mug before serving.   *Makes 8 servings*

Holiday Peppermint Bark

Mini Easter Tarts

1 (8-ounce) package cream cheese, softened
1 (14-ounce) can sweetened condensed milk
½ cup frozen lemonade concentrate, thawed
    Red, yellow or green food coloring, optional
1½ cups frozen whipped topping, thawed
2 (4-ounce) packages READY CRUST® Mini-Graham
    Cracker Crusts
    Fresh sliced fruit or assorted candies

1. Beat cream cheese in large bowl until fluffy. Gradually beat in sweetened condensed milk until smooth. Stir in lemonade concentrate. Add food coloring, if desired. Gently stir in whipped topping. Spoon into crusts.

2. Chill 3 hours.

3. Top with fruit or candies. Refrigerate leftovers.

Makes 12 servings

Prep Time: 10 minutes
Chilling Time: 3 hours

Orange Pecan Pie

3 eggs
½ cup GRANDMA'S® Molasses
½ cup light corn syrup
¼ cup orange juice
1 teaspoon grated orange peel
1 teaspoon vanilla
1½ cups whole pecan halves
1 (9-inch) unbaked pie shell
    Whipped cream (optional)

Heat oven to 350°F. In large bowl, beat eggs. Add molasses, corn syrup, orange juice, orange peel and vanilla; beat until well blended. Stir in pecans. Pour into unbaked pie shell. Bake 30 to 45 minutes or until filling sets. Cool on wire rack. Garnish as desired. Serve with whipped cream, if desired.

Makes 8 servings

Holiday Fanfare

Mini Easter Tarts

Gingered Pumpkin Custard

¾ **cup sugar**
2 **eggs**
1½ **teaspoons ground cinnamon**
½ **teaspoon salt**
½ **teaspoon ground nutmeg**
1 **can (15 ounces) solid-pack pumpkin**
1¼ **cups half-and-half**
3 **tablespoons chopped candied ginger**
Sweetened whipped cream
Halloween sprinkles or candy corn

1. Preheat oven to 375°F. Grease 1½-quart casserole or 8-inch glass baking dish.

2. Combine sugar, eggs, cinnamon, salt and nutmeg in medium bowl; mix well. Add pumpkin and half-and-half. Mix until well blended. Pour into prepared dish. Sprinkle ginger evenly over top of pumpkin mixture.

3. Bake 45 minutes or until knife inserted in center comes out clean. Cool on wire rack at least 20 minutes before serving. Serve warm or at room temperature. Garnish with whipped cream and sprinkles.

Makes 6 to 8 servings

Variation: For individual servings, pour custard mixture into 6 or 8 ramekins or custard cups. Place on a baking sheet. Bake 35 to 40 minutes or until knife inserted in center comes out clean.

Tasty Tip

Candied (or crystallized) ginger has been cooked in a sugar syrup and coated with coarse sugar. Although the candied ginger provides the uniquely special taste to this pumpkin dessert, 2 to 3 teaspoons ground ginger can be substituted, if necessary.

Gingered Pumpkin Custard

Mini Pumpkin Cranberry Breads

3 cups all-purpose flour
1 tablespoon plus 2 teaspoons pumpkin pie spice
2 teaspoons baking soda
1½ teaspoons salt
3 cups granulated sugar
1 can (15 ounces) LIBBY'S® 100% Pure Pumpkin
4 large eggs
1 cup vegetable oil
½ cup orange juice or water
1 cup sweetened dried, fresh or frozen cranberries

PREHEAT oven to 350°F. Grease and flour five or six 5×3-inch mini disposable loaf pans.

COMBINE flour, pumpkin pie spice, baking soda and salt in large bowl. Combine sugar, pumpkin, eggs, vegetable oil and orange juice in large mixer bowl; beat until just blended. Add pumpkin mixture to flour mixture; stir just until moistened. Fold in cranberries. Spoon batter into prepared loaf pans.

BAKE for 50 to 55 minutes or until wooden pick inserted in center comes out clean. Cool in pans on wire racks for 10 minutes; remove to wire racks to cool completely.   *Makes 5 or 6 mini loaves*

Miniature breads are perfect food gifts for holidays and special occasions. Wrap cooled mini loaves in aluminum or plastic wrap and tie with beautiful ribbons. Fill gift baskets with packages of speciality coffees or teas for heartwarming gifts straight from your kitchen.

Mini Pumpkin Cranberry Bread

Poinsettia Pie

2 cups chocolate wafer crumbs
6 tablespoons butter, melted
⅛ teaspoon peppermint extract (optional)
¾ cup sugar, divided
1 envelope unflavored gelatin
⅓ cup cold water
3 eggs, separated*
⅓ cup créme de menthe
½ cup whipping cream, whipped
   Chocolate Leaves (page 130)
1 round yellow candy

*Use only grade A clean, uncracked eggs.

1. Preheat oven to 350°F. Combine cookie crumbs, butter and peppermint extract, if desired, in small bowl. Press onto bottom and up side of 9-inch pie plate. Bake 8 minutes. Cool on wire rack.

2. Combine ½ cup sugar and gelatin in small saucepan. Add cold water; let stand 1 minute. Stir over low heat until gelatin is completely dissolved.

3. Beat egg yolks in small bowl. Stir about ¼ cup gelatin mixture into egg yolks; return egg yolk mixture to saucepan. Cook over low heat, stirring constantly, until thick enough to coat back of spoon. Remove from heat; stir in liqueur. Cool to room temperature.

4. Beat egg whites until foamy. Gradually beat in remaining ¼ cup sugar; continue beating until soft peaks form. Fold into gelatin mixture. Gently fold in whipped cream. Pour into cooled crust. Refrigerate until firm, 8 hours or overnight.

5. Prepare Chocolate Leaves, reserving small amount of melted chocolate.

6. Arrange Chocolate Leaves on pie to create poinsettia, using reserved chocolate to attach leaves. Place yellow candy in center. Refrigerate until serving time.   *Makes 1 (9-inch) pie*

Poinsettia Pie

Chocolate Leaves

Ingredients
¾ cup coarsely chopped white chocolate baking bars
or confectionery coating
Red food coloring
Shortening
¾ cup coarsely chopped semisweet chocolate

Supplies
Pastry brush
6 to 8 medium and 4 to 5 large lemon leaves*

These non-toxic leaves are available in florist shops.

1. Melt white chocolate in top of double boiler over hot, not boiling water, stirring constantly. Stir in red food coloring, a few drops at a time, until desired shade is reached. If chocolate begins to thicken or loses its shine, stir in shortening, 1 teaspoon at a time.

2. Brush thin layer of pink chocolate on back side of each medium-sized leaf with pastry brush. Do not spread to edge of leaf. Place on waxed paper-lined baking sheet. Refrigerate about 30 minutes or until firm.

3. Repeat with semisweet chocolate and large leaves, omitting food coloring. Refrigerate about 30 minutes or until firm.

4. Gently peel leaves off chocolate, beginning at stem ends. Refrigerate until ready to use.

You'll be the star of the event when you bring a fancy decorated pie. Decorating with chocolate leaves makes a very impressive gift. Be sure to select non-toxic leaves. Then, let your creativity go wild!

Pistachio Cookie Cups

½ cup (1 stick) plus 1 tablespoon butter, softened and divided
1 package (3 ounces) cream cheese, softened
2 tablespoons granulated sugar
1 cup all-purpose flour
½ teaspoon grated orange peel
1 cup powdered sugar
½ cup chopped pistachio nuts
⅓ cup dried cranberries
1 egg
½ teaspoon orange extract

1. Beat ½ cup butter, cream cheese and granulated sugar in medium bowl at medium speed of electric mixer until light and fluffy. Add flour and orange peel; beat until just blended. Shape into ball; wrap in plastic wrap. Freeze 30 minutes.

2. Combine all remaining ingredients in small bowl; mix well. Set aside.

3. Preheat oven to 350°F. Lightly spray 24 mini muffin cups with nonstick cooking spray.

4. Press 1 tablespoon dough firmly into bottom and up side of each muffin cup. Fill shells ¾ full with pistachio mixture.

5. Bake 25 minutes or until filling is set. Remove cookie cups to wire rack; cool completely. Sprinkle with additional powdered sugar, if desired.   *Makes 2 dozen cookies*

Holiday Cheese Tarts

1 (8-ounce) package cream cheese, softened
1 (14-ounce) can EAGLE BRAND® Sweetened Condensed Milk
    (NOT evaporated milk)
⅓ cup lemon juice from concentrate
1 teaspoon vanilla extract
2 (4-ounce) packages single-serve graham cracker crumb pie
    crusts
    Assorted fruit (strawberries, blueberries, bananas, raspberries,
    orange segments, cherries, kiwi fruit, grapes, pineapple, etc.)
¼ cup apple jelly, melted (optional)

1. In medium mixing bowl, beat cream cheese until fluffy. Gradually beat in EAGLE BRAND® until smooth. Stir in lemon juice and vanilla.

2. Spoon into crusts. Chill 2 hours or until set. Just before serving, top with fruit; brush with jelly (optional). Refrigerate leftovers.

Makes 12 tarts

Prep Time: 10 minutes
Chill Time: 2 hours

Tasty Tip

If you want to trim the fat in any Eagle Brand® recipe, just use Eagle Brand® Fat Free or Low Fat Sweetened Condensed Milk instead of the original Eagle Brand.®

Holiday Cheese Tarts

Decadent Truffle Tree

Ingredients
1⅓ cups whipping cream
¼ cup packed brown sugar
¼ cup light rum
2 teaspoons vanilla
¼ teaspoon salt
16 ounces semisweet chocolate, chopped
16 ounces milk chocolate, chopped
    Finely chopped nuts and assorted sprinkles

Supplies
1 (9-inch tall) foam cone
    About 70 wooden toothpicks

1. Heat cream, sugar, rum, vanilla and salt in medium saucepan over medium heat until sugar is dissolved and mixture is hot. Remove from heat; add chocolates, stirring until melted (return pan to low heat if necessary). Pour into shallow dish. Cover and refrigerate until just firm, about 1 hour.

2. Shape about half the mixture into 1¼-inch balls. Shape remaining mixture into ¾-inch balls. Roll balls in nuts and sprinkles. Refrigerate truffles until firm, about 1 hour.

3. Cover cone with foil. Starting at bottom of cone, attach larger truffles with toothpicks. Use smaller truffles toward the top of the cone. Refrigerate until serving time.   *Makes 1 tree (6 dozen truffles)*

Note: If kitchen is very warm, keep portion of truffle mixture chilled as you shape and roll balls.

Festive Holiday Punch

8 cups MOTT'S® Apple Juice
8 cups cranberry juice cocktail
2 red apples, sliced
2 cups cranberries
3 liters lemon-lime soda
    Ice cubes, as needed

Pour apple and cranberry juices into punch bowl. Fifteen minutes before serving, add apple slices, cranberries, soda and ice. Do not stir.
Makes 24 servings

Decadent Truffle Tree

Outrageous Pajama Parties

Creamy Artichoke-Parmesan Dip

2 cans (14 ounces each) artichoke hearts, drained and chopped
2 cups (8 ounces) shredded mozzarella cheese
1½ cups grated Parmesan cheese
1½ cups mayonnaise
½ cup finely chopped onion
½ teaspoon dried oregano leaves
¼ teaspoon garlic powder
4 pita breads
   Assorted cut-up vegetables

Slow Cooker Directions

1. Combine artichokes, cheeses, mayonnaise, onion, oregano and garlic powder in slow cooker; mix well.

2. Cover; cook on LOW 2 hours.

3. Meanwhile, cut pita breads into wedges. Arrange pita breads and vegetables on platter; serve with warm dip.   *Makes 4 cups dip*

Creamy Artichoke-Parmesan Dip

Cranberry Gorp

¼ cup (½ stick) butter
¼ cup packed light brown sugar
1 tablespoon maple syrup
1 teaspoon curry powder
½ teaspoon ground cinnamon
1½ cups dried cranberries
1½ cups coarsely chopped walnuts and/or slivered almonds
1½ cups lightly salted pretzel nuggets

1. Preheat oven to 300°F. Grease 15×10-inch jelly-roll pan. Combine butter, brown sugar and maple syrup in large saucepan; heat over medium heat until butter is melted. Stir in curry powder and cinnamon. Add cranberries, walnuts and pretzels; stir to combine.

2. Spread mixture on prepared pan. Bake 15 minutes or until mixture is crunchy and light brown.   *Makes 20 servings*

Cucumber-Dill Dip

Salt
1 cucumber, peeled, seeded and finely chopped
6 green onions, white parts only, chopped
1 cup plain yogurt
1 package (3 ounces) cream cheese
2 tablespoons fresh dill *or* 1 tablespoon dried dill weed
Vegetable dippers

1. Lightly salt cucumber in small bowl; toss. Refrigerate 1 hour. Drain cucumber; dry on paper towels. Return cucumbers to bowl and add onions. Set aside.

2. Place yogurt, cream cheese and dill in food processor or blender; process until smooth. Stir into cucumber mixture. Cover; refrigerate 1 hour. Serve with vegetable dippers.   *Makes about 2 cups dip*

Cranberry Gorp

Fresh Fruit with Creamy Lime Dipping Sauce

1 small jicama, peeled and cut into ½-inch-thick strips
2 tablespoons lime juice
2 pounds watermelon, rind removed, cut into ½-inch-thick
    wedges
½ small pineapple, peeled, halved lengthwise and cut crosswise
    into wedges
1 ripe papaya, peeled, seeded and sliced crosswise
    Creamy Lime Dipping Sauce (recipe follows)

Combine jicama and lime juice in large bowl; toss. Drain. Arrange
jicama, watermelon, pineapple and papaya on large platter. Serve with
Creamy Lime Dipping Sauce. Garnish as desired.

Makes 12 servings

Creamy Lime Dipping Sauce

1 carton (6 ounces) vanilla-flavored yogurt
2 tablespoons minced fresh cilantro
2 tablespoons lime juice
1 tablespoon minced jalapeño pepper*

**Jalapeño peppers can sting and irritate the skin; wear rubber gloves when handling peppers and do
not touch eyes. Wash hands after handling.*

Combine all ingredients in small bowl; mix well to combine.

Makes about 1 cup

Chocolate Almond Cherry Mix

2 cups toasted almonds
2 cups red and green candy coated chocolate pieces
2 cups dried cherries

Combine all ingredients in large bowl; mix well.

Makes 6 cups

Fresh Fruit with Creamy Lime Dipping Sauce

Pepperoni-Oregano Focaccia

1 tablespoon cornmeal
1 can (10 ounces) refrigerated pizza crust dough
½ cup finely chopped pepperoni (3 to 3½ ounces)
1½ teaspoons finely chopped fresh oregano *or* ½ teaspoon
    dried oregano leaves
2 teaspoons olive oil

1. Preheat oven to 425°F. Grease large baking sheet; sprinkle with cornmeal. Set aside.

2. Unroll dough on lightly floured surface. Pat dough into 12×9-inch rectangle. Sprinkle half the pepperoni and half the oregano over one side of dough. Fold over dough, making 12×4½-inch rectangle.

3. Roll dough into 12×9-inch rectangle. Place on prepared baking sheet. Prick dough with fork at 2-inch intervals about 30 times. Brush with oil; sprinkle with remaining pepperoni and oregano.

4. Bake 12 to 15 minutes or until golden brown. (Prick dough several more times if dough puffs as it bakes.) Cut into strips.

Makes 12 servings

Everything Ham Dip

1 (3-ounce) package cream cheese, softened
½ cup sour cream
1 tablespoon sherry
1 (5-ounce) can HORMEL® Chunk Ham, drained and flaked
2 tablespoons chopped water chestnuts
2 tablespoons minced onion
½ teaspoon dried dill weed
3 slices bacon, cooked and crumbled
3 tablespoons finely chopped pecans
    Melba toast, if desired

Beat cream cheese until light and fluffy. Add sour cream and sherry. Beat until smooth. Stir in ham, water chestnuts, onion and dill weed. Cover and refrigerate until chilled, about 1 hour. Stir in bacon and pecans just before serving. Serve with melba toast, if desired.

Makes about 2 cups

Pepperoni-Oregano Focaccia

Rosemary-Scented Nut Mix

2 tablespoons butter
2 cups pecan halves
1 cup unsalted macadamia nuts
1 cup walnuts
1 teaspoon dried rosemary, crushed
½ teaspoon salt
¼ teaspoon red pepper flakes

1. Preheat oven to 300°F. Melt butter in large saucepan over low heat. Add pecans, macadamia nuts and walnuts; mix well. Add rosemary, salt and red pepper flakes; cook and stir about 1 minute.

2. Pour mixture onto ungreased nonstick baking sheet. Bake 15 minutes, stirring mixture occasionally. Let cool completely.

Makes 32 servings

Caramel Apple Wedges

⅔ cup sugar
¼ cup (½ stick) butter, cut into small pieces
½ cup whipping cream
¼ teaspoon salt
3 apples, cored, cut into 6 wedges each
½ cup shredded coconut
¼ cup mini chocolate chips

1. Place sugar in medium, heavy saucepan. Cook over low heat until sugar melts, about 20 minutes. Carefully stir in butter. Gradually stir in cream. (Mixture will spatter.) Cook over low heat until any lumps disappear, about 15 minutes, stirring occasionally. Stir in salt.

2. To serve, pour caramel sauce into serving bowl or fondue pot over heat source. Arrange apple wedges on a plate. Combine coconut and chocolate chips in separate serving dish.

3. Using fondue forks, dip apple wedges into caramel sauce, then into coconut mixture.

Makes 6 servings

Variation: To make caramel apples, combine 1 package (14 ounces) caramels and 2 tablespoons water in heavy saucepan. Melt over low heat, about 10 minutes. Roll apples in melted caramel mixture, then in coconut-chocolate chip mixture. Cool on sheet of waxed paper until firm.

Rosemary-Scented Nut Mix

Zesty Pesto Cheese Spread and Dip

2 packages (8 ounces each) cream cheese, softened
1 cup shredded mozzarella cheese
1 cup chopped fresh basil or parsley
½ cup grated Parmesan cheese
½ cup pine nuts, toasted
⅓ cup *French's*® *Gourmayo*™ Sun Dried Tomato Light Mayonnaise
1 teaspoon minced garlic

1. Combine all ingredients in food processor. Cover and process until smooth and well blended.

2. Spoon pesto spread into serving bowl or crock. Spread on crackers or serve with vegetable crudités.   *Makes 12 (¼-cup) servings*

Tip: To toast pine nuts, place nuts on baking sheet. Bake at 350°F for 8 to 10 minutes or until lightly golden or microwave on HIGH (100%) 1 minute.

Serving Suggestion: Use Pesto Spread as a filling in sandwich wraps or pipe into cherry tomatoes using a pastry bag filled with a decorative tip.

Prep Time: 15 minutes

Fiesta Dip

1 package (1 ounce) LAWRY'S® Taco Spices & Seasonings
2 cups sour cream
   Tortilla chips and assorted crisp vegetables

In medium bowl, combine Taco Spices & Seasonings with sour cream; mix thoroughly. Cover and refrigerate for about 1 hour. Serve with tortilla chips and crisp vegetables.   *Makes 2 cups*

Variation: Also makes a great spread on flour tortillas when making wraps. Simply spread over surface of tortilla, add fillings and roll-up.

Prep Time: 3 minutes

Zesty Pesto Cheese Spread and Dip

Wisconsin Gouda and Beer Spread

2 pounds Wisconsin Gouda Cheese*
¾ cup butter, cubed and softened
2 tablespoons snipped fresh chives
2 teaspoons Dijon mustard
½ cup amber ale, at room temperature
Cocktail rye or pumpernickel bread slices

*Cut ⅓ from top of cheese to create flat surface. With butter curler or melon baller, remove cheese from center of ball leaving ½-inch-thick shell. Shred enough of cheese removed from ball and top to measure 4 cups. Reserve remaining cheese for another use.

In large bowl, place shredded cheese, butter, chives and mustard; mix with spoon until blended. Stir in beer until blended. Spoon spread into hollowed cheese ball; reserve remaining spread for refills. Chill until serving time. Serve with cocktail bread. **Makes 4 cups**

Tip: Cut the opening at the top of the cheese in a decorative pattern.

Favorite recipe from **Wisconsin Milk Marketing Board**

Crispy Bacon Sticks

½ cup (1½ ounces) grated Wisconsin Parmesan cheese, divided
5 slices bacon, halved lengthwise
10 breadsticks

Microwave Directions

Spread ¼ cup cheese on plate. Press one side of bacon into cheese; wrap diagonally around breadstick with cheese-coated side toward stick. Place on paper plate or microwave-safe baking sheet lined with paper towels. Repeat with remaining bacon halves, cheese and breadsticks. Microwave on HIGH 4 to 6 minutes until bacon is cooked, checking for doneness after 4 minutes. Roll again in remaining ¼ cup Parmesan cheese. Serve warm. **Makes 10 sticks**

Favorite recipe from **Wisconsin Milk Marketing Board**

Wisconsin Gouda and Beer Spread

Antipasto Crescent Bites

2 ounces cream cheese (do not use reduced-fat or fat-free
    cream cheese)
1 package (8 ounces) refrigerated crescent roll dough
1 egg plus 1 tablespoon water, beaten
16 strips roasted red pepper, 3×¾ inch long
2 large marinated artichoke hearts, cut in half lengthwise
1 thin slice Genoa or other salami, cut into 4 strips
4 small stuffed green olives, cut into halves

1. Preheat oven to 375°F. Cut cream cheese into 16 equal pieces, about 1 teaspoon per piece; set aside.

2. Remove dough from package. Unroll on lightly floured surface. Cut each triangle of dough in half to form 2 triangles. Brush outer edges of triangle lightly with egg mixture.

3. Wrap 1 pepper strip around 1 piece of cream cheese. Place on dough triangle. Fold over and pinch edges to seal; repeat with remaining pepper strips. Place 1 piece artichoke heart and 1 piece of cream cheese on dough triangle. Fold over and pinch edges to seal; repeat with remaining pieces of artichoke hearts. Wrap 1 strip salami around 1 piece of cream cheese. Place on dough triangle. Fold over and pinch edges to seal; repeat with remaining salami. Place 2 olive halves and 1 piece of cream cheese on dough triangle. Fold over and pinch edges to seal; repeat with remaining olives. Place evenly spaced on ungreased baking sheet. Brush with egg mixture.

4. Bake 12 to 14 minutes or until golden brown. Serve warm.

Makes 16 pieces

Tip: Bites may be made ahead. Cool on wire rack and store in airtight container in refrigerator. To serve, reheat on baking sheet in preheated 325°F oven 7 to 8 minutes or until warmed through. Do not microwave.

Antipasto Crescent Bites

Texas Pecan and Beef Dip

½ cup pecan pieces
3 tablespoons thinly sliced green onions with tops
1 package (8 ounces) cream cheese, softened and cut into cubes
3 ounces lager beer
½ jar (2.2 ounces) dried beef, rinsed in hot water, drained and
    cut into ¼-inch pieces
1½ teaspoons BBQ seasoning blend
    Breadsticks, pita bread and assorted fresh vegetables for
    dipping

1. Spray bottom of small saucepan generously with nonstick cooking spray; heat over medium heat until hot. Add pecans and onions; cook over medium heat 3 to 5 minutes or until pecans are toasted and onions are tender.

2. Add cream cheese and lager to saucepan; cook over medium-low heat until cheese is melted. Stir in dried beef and BBQ seasoning; cook over medium-high heat, stirring constantly, until hot.

3. Spoon dip into bowl; sprinkle with additional green onion tops, if desired. Serve with dippers. *Makes 8 (3-tablespoon) servings*

Prep and Cook Time: 18 minutes

Hotsy Totsy Spiced Nuts

1 can (12 ounces) mixed nuts
3 tablespoons *Frank's® RedHot®* Original Cayenne Pepper Sauce
1 tablespoon vegetable oil
¾ teaspoon seasoned salt
¾ teaspoon garlic powder

1. Preheat oven to 250°F. Place nuts in 10×15-inch jelly-roll pan. Combine remaining ingredients in small bowl; pour over nuts. Toss to coat evenly.

2. Bake 45 minutes or until nuts are toasted and dry, stirring every 15 minutes. Cool completely. *Makes about 2 cups mix*

Prep Time: 5 minutes
Cook Time: 45 minutes

Texas Pecan and Beef Dip

Acknowledgments

The publisher would like to thank the companies and organizations listed below for the use of their recipes and photographs in this publication.

Bays English Muffin Corporation

BelGioioso® Cheese, Inc.

Cherry Marketing Institute

Crisco is a registered trademark of The J.M. Smucker Company

Duncan Hines® and Moist Deluxe® are registered trademarks of Pinnacle Foods Corp.

Eagle Brand® Sweetened Condensed Milk

Grandma's® is a registered trademark of Mott's, LLP

Hershey Foods Corporation

Hormel Foods, Carapelli USA, LLC and Melting Pot Foods Inc.

Hormel Foods, LLC

Jennie-O Turkey Store®

Kahlúa® Liqueur

Keebler® Company

Lawry's® Foods

Mott's® is a registered trademark of Mott's, LLP

National Honey Board

National Turkey Federation

Nestlé USA

Perdue Farms Incorporated

Reckitt Benckiser Inc.

StarKist Seafood Company

Unilever Foods North America

Wisconsin Milk Marketing Board

Index

Metric Conversion Chart

VOLUME MEASUREMENTS (dry)

1/8 teaspoon = 0.5 mL
1/4 teaspoon = 1 mL
1/2 teaspoon = 2 mL
3/4 teaspoon = 4 mL
1 teaspoon = 5 mL
1 tablespoon = 15 mL
2 tablespoons = 30 mL
1/4 cup = 60 mL
1/3 cup = 75 mL
1/2 cup = 125 mL
2/3 cup = 150 mL
3/4 cup = 175 mL
1 cup = 250 mL
2 cups = 1 pint = 500 mL
3 cups = 750 mL
4 cups = 1 quart = 1 L

VOLUME MEASUREMENTS (fluid)

1 fluid ounce (2 tablespoons) = 30 mL
4 fluid ounces (1/2 cup) = 125 mL
8 fluid ounces (1 cup) = 250 mL
12 fluid ounces (1 1/2 cups) = 375 mL
16 fluid ounces (2 cups) = 500 mL

WEIGHTS (mass)

1/2 ounce = 15 g
1 ounce = 30 g
3 ounces = 90 g
4 ounces = 120 g
8 ounces = 225 g
10 ounces = 285 g
12 ounces = 360 g
16 ounces = 1 pound = 450 g

DIMENSIONS

1/16 inch = 2 mm
1/8 inch = 3 mm
1/4 inch = 6 mm
1/2 inch = 1.5 cm
3/4 inch = 2 cm
1 inch = 2.5 cm

OVEN TEMPERATURES

250°F = 120°C
275°F = 140°C
300°F = 150°C
325°F = 160°C
350°F = 180°C
375°F = 190°C
400°F = 200°C
425°F = 220°C
450°F = 230°C

BAKING PAN SIZES

Utensil	Size in Inches/Quarts	Metric Volume	Size in Centimeters
Baking or Cake Pan (square or rectangular)	8×8×2	2 L	20×20×5
	9×9×2	2.5 L	23×23×5
	12×8×2	3 L	30×20×5
	13×9×2	3.5 L	33×23×5
Loaf Pan	8×4×3	1.5 L	20×10×7
	9×5×3	2 L	23×13×7
Round Layer Cake Pan	8×1½	1.2 L	20×4
	9×1½	1.5 L	23×4
Pie Plate	8×1¼	750 mL	20×3
	9×1¼	1 L	23×3
Baking Dish or Casserole	1 quart	1 L	—
	1½ quart	1.5 L	—
	2 quart	2 L	—

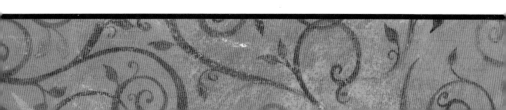